Mourning the Dreams
How Parents Create Meaning from Miscarriage, Stillbirth and Early Infant Death

by

Claudia Malacrida

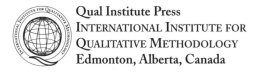
Qual Institute Press
INTERNATIONAL INSTITUTE FOR
QUALITATIVE METHODOLOGY
Edmonton, Alberta, Canada

For information:

Qual Institute Press
INTERNATIONAL INSTITUTE FOR
QUALITATIVE METHODOLOGY
Sixth Floor
University Extension Centre
8303–112th Street
University of Alberta
Edmonton, Alberta, Canada T6G 2T4
Phone: 1-403-492-9041
Fax: 1-403-492-9040
Email: qualitative.institute@ualberta.ca
Or order books from our website: http://www.ualberta.ca/~iiqm/

Printed in Canada

Canadian Cataloging-in-Publication Data

Malacrida, Claudia, Date
      Mourning the dreams: how parents make meaning from miscarriage,
      stillbirth and early infant death
      Includes bibliographical references and indexes.
      ISBN 0-9683044-0-0
      1. Perinatal death—Psychological aspects. 2. Bereavement—
      Psychological aspects. I. Title.
      BF575.G7M19 1998   155.9'37'085   C98-900171-7

Editor:	Janice M. Morse
Managing Editor:	Don Wells
Graphic Design:	Murray Pearson
Front Cover Artwork:	Barbara Bickel
Back Cover Photo:	Hilary Malacrida

Contents

DEDICATION

For the babies,
who taught us so much in such a short time.

Acknowledgements

I have been privileged in a number of ways while conducting this research. People were extremely generous in sharing their experiences of losing a baby prematurely or at term. The overarching desire of participants to speak their piece, share their knowledge, and improve the plight of others meant that they were willing to be intimate and open with me. I am honored to have heard their stories.

I have also been very fortunate in the mentorship of my thesis supervisor, Dr. Arthur Frank. His knowledge and willingness to allow me to take risks provided an extremely conducive working environment. His wisdom and insight have enriched my creativity and improved my critical thinking. It has been a rare gift to work with such a mentor.

I appreciate the assistance I received from volunteers at Caring Beyond and from members of the support group in Medicine Hat, particularly from Sherry Kopp, who organized my interviews and group sessions in that town. I also am grateful for Susan Ruttan of the *Calgary Herald*, whose call for participants facilitated my research so well. The thesis research grant I received from the University of Calgary Research Grants Committee and the research scholarships I received from the Department of Sociology were also very helpful.

Finally, I must thank my husband, Carey Malacrida, and my daughter, Hilary Malacrida. They have sacrificed a lot of picnics and family fun times to accommodate the research and writing of this work. They also lived through the dark times of my coming to terms with the material and with our own losses. Further, they have done so with good humour and great love. I am blessed.

Preface
The Quest Begins

Perinatal loss includes infant death from pregnancy complications, prematurity, stillbirth, or complications within the first month of life. For parents, recovering from the loss of a child perinatally can be extremely difficult. Parents often find their personal experiences at odds with prevailing ideas and assumptions. They are placed in a position of having to justify their feelings in the face of denial and silence from friends, family, their religious communities, their workplaces, the medical community, and even within their marital relationships. Sometimes, bereaved parents themselves fail to see their feelings of grief as legitimate or normal. This study seeks to understand how parents who have suffered the death of a child through perinatal loss come to create meaning from their losses, despite nonlegitimating social influences and the parents' own intra-psychic pressures to minimize their grief.

It is important for me to explain my interest in and approach to the study of this topic. The construction of any research work inevitably bears the mark of the person who created it, affecting both how the research is designed and the level of understanding that can be attempted in its study (Riessman, 1993). Research on emotions and lived emotional experience, such as the loss of a child and the negotiation of meaning from that loss, require special understanding and knowledge. A number of researchers in the sociology of the emotions have called for "emotional research" that begins with a biographically subjective experience on the part of the researcher and then moves to a theoretical level of abstraction (Denzin, 1989; Ellis, 1991). Ellis (1991) argues that this approach will "offer a more holistic understanding of emotions and a fuller appreciation for how emotional experience is connected to other dimensions of human life" (p. 125). I am seeking to understand this very connection between private loss and other dimensions of human life such as public acknowledgement, social support and prevailing social norms. The foundation of my inquiry is my own experience. Not only am I a social researcher, but I am a woman who has herself suffered through perinatal loss.

On March 1, 1989, after nearly a month of agonizing uncertainty, my daughter, Victoria Ann, was delivered, still, at the age of five months. I had lain in the hospital off and on for a month, being checked with fetal monitors, having ultrasounds, worrying about my then 4-year-old daughter, fretting over my then 3-year-old business, watching my life crumble around me. During the time I was losing Victoria, I busied myself with arranging childcare for my daughter, notifying grandparents, arranging staffing at my business, trying to sustain a normal flow to my life. I even had my suppliers haul racks of clothing into the hospital so that I could buy Fall inventory for the women's boutique I owned at the time. Before I actually lost Victoria, I acted as though nothing major was happening. It was as if by doing what I always did—being a mother, managing a home, running a business, keeping in touch with friends and family—I hoped to take out some "psychological insurance" on a normal life. It was my way of bargaining for a swift return to who I was before, with only a month taken out of my life, and a small sadness to remind me of what had been lost.

After all the pressure, I expected Victoria's death would come as a release. After all, she could not have survived, and if she was not going to survive, then logic would dictate that the best thing to do would be to get on with the rest of my, of our, lives. The afternoon she died, a girlfriend stopped in on her way to dinner, arriving just in time to be with me while I gave birth. I remember she cried when she saw Victoria and that I felt surprised that she should feel so moved.

The day after Victoria's death, I was back at work, in the business I had always referred to as "my second child." Oddly, everything that had sustained me through her loss seemed of little interest. The business I had so passionately clung to, the friends and lifestyle I had valued so highly seemed perfectly disposable the night my husband came home and said he had a possibility of transferring to Calgary, a place we had never been. Within a month, we had closed out the business, said goodbye to our friends and acquaintances, and were on our way to a new beginning.

I began working in a low-stress job, chosen precisely because it would accommodate pregnancy and childrearing. We slowly established ourselves in our new home, formed tentative friendships, and began to feel cautious optimism. I became pregnant. On May 11, 1990, I lost our son, Evan Thomas, at 26 weeks. He lived for an hour or so, and with his death, a part of me died, too.

With nowhere to run, nowhere to hide, I was forced to face my demons. Only in adolescence have I felt so cut adrift from myself, from others. Everything that I knew about myself became questionable. I had always defined myself as capable, nurturing, self-knowing, and resilient, yet these were the very qualities that were failing me. I was not capable; I had failed the most fundamental task of womanhood. I was not nurturing; I could not even carry my babies to term. I was not self-knowing; I was swept away, unprepared for the depth of my feelings. And I certainly was not resilient because as my sadness wore on and as others seemed to forget or move on with their lives, I suspected I was failing at grieving, too.

Eventually, I returned to school, studying psychology and counselling. I began working with AIDS victims, refugees, and battered women. After all, I knew about pain. Victoria and Evan died for something, even it was only so that I could be wiser, more educated and useful to others. My education and my public service became ways for me to salvage some purpose out of my loss. It was only six years later, in graduate school, that I felt prepared to work directly on the topic closest to my heart.

When I told those near to me that I had decided to do my thesis on late-term miscarriage and stillbirth, the response was not supportive. Many people expressed concern that by doing this study I would be stirring things up again and that to do so would cause pain to myself and those I loved. Others did not respond at all, changing the subject or terminating the conversation adroitly. No one acknowledged that this was a very interesting and worthwhile topic and that I would certainly be able to bring insight to its study.

I felt that I was treading on dangerous ground. I was contravening the dictates of common sense by flirting with emotions best left alone. I was contravening the dictates of common decency by remaining obsessed with something that should be well past by now.

The time, however, was right. I believed that I was distanced enough from the pain to be able to "handle" the feelings that this research might refresh. I also believed that this distance would enable me to focus my research efforts on the stories of others rather than on my own story alone. I acknowledged that my six years of self-reflection would inevitably affect the research; however, I felt that the inclusion of my subjective insight and lived experience in the research would enrich and broaden the study rather than hamper its accuracy. I believed that my own experience would add to, rather than conflict with, my understanding of how parents create meaning from their experiences of perinatal loss.

Chapter 1
Why is Perinatal Loss So Painful?

Before attempting to understand how parents create sense or meaning out of their losses, I felt it was critical to understand the nature of those losses. What is it about perinatal loss that is so powerful? What is particular to perinatal loss that makes grief so poignant and recovery so difficult? My search of the literature was extensive—I found insights that fleshed out the answers to these questions in medical sociology, in thanatology, in the sociology of the emotions, in social work and psychology, in feminist writing, and in medical books on the topic. As discussed below, I have borrowed from all of these traditions, but particularly I have used Kenneth J. Doka's (1987, 1989) work on disenfranchised grief and Therese A. Rando's (1984, 1992, 1993) work on complicated mourning as a model to guide my inquiry.

It is important for me to note that part of my desire to do this research rested on my personal need for legitimation—my own need to know that my experience was not abnormal. In undertaking this project, I felt a compelling need to find something outside of myself that might account for the devastation I experienced. My fear was that if I failed to find anything in the varied bodies of literature I explored that would illuminate the complexity and profundity of perinatal loss the logical conclusion would be that there was something wrong with me for having been so deeply affected by my losses. My literature search on the topic led me to conclude that in fact little has been written that directly explains the breadth and depth of perinatal grief adequately. Subsequently, I have drawn on a wide-ranging variety of sources to guide my thinking.

PERINATAL LOSS LITERATURE

Literature dealing directly with perinatal loss generally falls into two categories: medical approaches and mental health treatments. Medical approaches toward perinatal loss often make recommendations to caregivers on how best to "manage" the loss experience within the hospital setting. These recommendations include providing as many infant artifacts as possible, encouraging contact with the babies, providing extra hospital support for parents, and encouraging the study of long-term parental needs (Taner Leff, 1987, p. 111). Another medical approach describes normal and abnormal pregnancy, comparing abnormal pregnancies to normal ones, and explaining what can go wrong with a pregnancy. Some authors offer insight into what to expect physically and, to a lesser extent, emotionally following perinatal loss, ending with recommendations on how to proceed with subsequent pregnancies (Lovell, 1983; Oakley, McPherson, & Roberts, 1984; Schwiebert & Kirk, 1989). While this literature is extremely useful in answering parents' questions about why perinatal loss happens or how to reduce subsequent risks, it does little to shed light on the profound nature of postloss grief.

Mental health writing on perinatal loss does address the nature of parental grief following perinatal loss, yet often, it fails to provide an analysis of the particularities that contribute to that grief. Mental health research has assessed the sympathy of health professionals towards miscarriage patients (Hai & Sullivan, 1982/1983), the effects of attending support groups on specific measures of psychosocial adjustment (Videka-Sherman & Lieberman, 1985), the nature and efficacy of the therapeutic helping relationship within married couples (Smart, 1992), and the role of religious commitment in achieving psychological adjustment (Cook & Wimberly, 1983). Typically, articles conclude with or consist primarily of recommendations for therapeutic interventions that will facilitate parental grief resolution (for example, Malcolm & Wooten, 1984; Rappaport, 1981). Such recommendations often include many of the same measures called for in the medical literature (e.g., allowing time for parental contact with the infant, provision of infant artifacts) and often provide guidelines for caregivers on such topics as making funeral recommendations to parents, providing advice on autopsy decisions, and recommending follow-up counselling to bereaved parents.

The findings and recommendations of the mental health literature are no more to be faulted than those of the medical literature, yet they shed little light on why perinatal grief, in particular, requires such measures. The lack of social support in parents' normal support systems, the ambiguity of medical and institutional responses to the death, and the varied secondary losses that necessitate counselling are not laid out in great detail. Rather, therapeutic measures are recommended in response to clinical experiences that have simply indicated that bereaved parents need special attention.

Some social science research does provide insight into underlying assumptions regarding perinatal loss. Shulamit Reinharz (1988) has explored some of the crosscultural meanings that have been attributed to perinatal loss. These include views of miscarriage as a symbol of failed maternal virtue, of failed womanhood, and as a test of character. The implication is that women are held liable for pregnancy loss through their lack of virtue or their inadequacy as women and that failure to give birth to a living child is a lesson necessary to character development. Reinharz also provides an analysis of some ways that miscarriage lore may act to restrict women's activities and emotions. The inference is that mothers are responsible for pregnancy loss because they undertake too much (or not enough) activity or because they invest excessive (or insufficient) emotion in their pregnancies. In any case, the underlying message is that mothers somehow invite perinatal loss through their own failings.

Historical and cultural contexts of perinatal loss have been explored by Letherby (1993), who postulates that perinatal loss has become more difficult in modern culture. She argues that lower infant mortality rates mean that modern, Western women no longer expect their children to die and hence are willing to form bonds to them at earlier stages of life. At the same time, increased availability of reproductive control means women are now more likely to focus on choosing rather than preventing pregnancy, presumably resulting in less ambivalence when they become pregnant. Finally, the increasing medicalization of pregnancy and childbirth has meant that women expect the pregnancies that they do choose to end successfully. These factors together form a modern concept of pregnancy as a selectable, manageable, and predictable undertaking. This, in turn, fosters unrealistic expectations of success in reproductive matters (Letherby, 1993).

Miscarriage and stillbirth have also become medical events, reducing the support that might have occurred in the past when women were tended by other community members who likely understood their experience of loss either through their own miscarriages or by attending other women's losses (Letherby, 1993). Layne (1992, p. 34) explores the implications of new reproductive technologies such as pregnancy tests, ultrasounds and amniocentesis that offer "the scientific determination of pregnancy before the sensation of fetal movement" and facilitate earlier and earlier parent-infant bonding by determining the sex of children before birth and offering visual connections to the baby in utero. The promise of these technologies interacts with a general tendency of medicine and the media to underreport pregnancy loss and overreport technology's "miracle babies," leaving both physicians and parents feeling that "it is *they* (not the technologies) who have failed if a neonate dies" (Layne, 1992, pp. 33–37). The belief that pregnancy is now typically safe and successful, combined with the hospital experience of perinatal loss that isolates women from other community members who might share their experience, can leave parents with an understanding that theirs is a personal failing and a private misfortune.

Layne's (1990) anthropological approach describes pregnancy as a rite of passage and pregnancy loss as an incomplete rite of passage that leaves parents without any status as fathers or mothers. She sees this as a major thrust behind parent support groups' struggles to define the embryo, foetus, or neonate as a child, in opposition to medical ascriptions of their infants as "fetal waste" or "products of conception." The struggle to define the baby as a real child is tied to struggles by mourners to claim the status of parents and to name their loss as a death. Layne points out that miscarried and stillborn babies are often not accorded funerals but continue to be disposed of by the hospital, a clear statement of the devalued status of perinatal deaths. For parents, this struggle is a social one, aimed at achieving acknowledgment and recognition that their status has indeed changed; they now are not only parents, but parents of a child who has died.

SOURCES OUTSIDE OF PERINATAL LOSS LITERATURE

Often, the topic of perinatal loss is subsumed in research that deals directly with other fields of study, again, without necessarily acknowledging the particularities that confront parents suffering through perinatal loss. Related sources include research on motherhood, the family, and pronatalism; thanatology; grief literature; and complicated mourning. Many of the themes in these research areas provide insight into why perinatal grief is problematic.

Motherhood, the family, and pronatalism

Literature dealing with the ideologies of the family can lend insight into why parents choose to have children, and hence, why losing a child can be so poignant. Rather than see motherhood as an instinctual drive, Elisabeth Badinter (1980), a French feminist historian, analyzes mothering practices across time. She ties the social imperative of "good mothering" to the publication of Rousseau's *Emile* and traces shifts in childrearing and burial practices to support her claims. Mother love as we presently know it is a social construct, shifting with the fashions of family structure across time and place (Badinter, 1980). In analyzing modern, Western attitudes towards children, Gittins (1993) believes that economic factors are not adequate explanations for bearing children; rather, she claims the bearing of children is a status passage; women only become "real" women, socially recognized as adults, when they become mothers. She also discusses the theme of power as a positive attribute of mothering, claiming that women in particular are often able to exercise power in only this area of their lives. Finally, parents desire children to "continue their line" and to provide some security (both financially and against loneliness) for themselves in old age. Logically, the loss of an infant could represent a loss of status as a "real" adults, loss of the potential power to be gained through mothering, loss of future comfort against loneliness, and loss of a route toward immortality through one's children (Gittins, 1993).

Veevers (1980) discusses some dominant cultural themes regarding family. In her study of couples who choose not to have children, she found many people encountered pronatalism. Pronatalism includes the belief that married people not only should have children, but should want to have them. The social meaning of parenthood is that being a parent is a highly moral activity; that being a parent is a civic responsibility; that parenthood is a part of being married; that desire for parenthood represents acceptance of one's gender role, that is, being a mother is proof of one's femininity; and finally, that desire for parenthood is a sign of normal mental health (Veevers, 1980, p. 4). With parenthood being so socially and morally charged, it is possible that "failed" parenthood will be interpreted in equally powerful terms both by parents and by those who surround them.

Thanatology

Thanatology, or the study of death, also sheds light indirectly on perinatal loss. A major theme in thanatology considers the denial and silence surrounding death in modern, Western culture, resulting in the fear and shame of death (Littlewood, 1993, p. 69). The old, Victorian ideal of the "good death," where the dying person, surrounded by loved ones, passed serenely over to a life of peace and joy at God's side, is gone. Victorian practices of mourning, which gave clear instructions about how, where, and when to mourn for all members of the community, have disappeared as well (Aries, 1985, p. 309). Mourners in modern times are left without internalized grieving rules and without public rituals to support and guide their feelings. In

6

the case of a perinatal death, there is even less public support for grief because the death of a yet-to-be-born child is not a "social death."

Social death refers to the loss of an individual to the community, to society, and to living others (Mulkay, 1993). A social death can be independent of a biological death, for example, when an ailing individual detaches more and more from his/her society and his/her presence (and hence loss) becomes increasingly less salient to community members. In a reversal of Mulkay's concept, the physical death of a preterm infant often occurs independently of a social death since a preterm infant is often socially salient only to parents. Thus, parental grief often occurs in a social vacuum, without the acknowledgement or support from others to whom the loss is not socially "real."

The configuration of the modern, nuclear family has also affected how one experiences grief. Because we live in a mobile, individualistic society, we are often situated in relatively few, intense relationships and have access to fewer and fewer people who share our stories, our joys, or our sorrows. As well, grief is often viewed as a private affair, so even in the case of social deaths, once the funeral is over, mourners are left with few supports for their grief (Charmaz, 1980, p. 281).

Studies focusing on children's deaths offer further insight into perinatal loss. As well as some of the more pronatalist or societal factors suggested above, there are some very personal and private reasons for parents to mourn the death of an infant. Children act as links to parents' own pasts and to their futures, providing insight into and forgiveness of one's own childhood while offering the promise that parents may be able to make amends or fulfill their dreams through their children (Arnold-Hagan & Buschman, 1983). With a baby (perhaps even more so with a yet-to-be-born baby), the struggles with and flaws of the actual child are not yet apparent, but the dream and the emotional investments remain. Arnold-Hagan and Buschman (1983) describe the parent-infant relationship as being particularly special, providing parents with the opportunity to give love unconditionally; to exercise control; to build self-esteem; to accomplish something meaningful; to have a reason to live; and, finally, to have something that is solely one's own. The death of an infant robs parents of these opportunities, dreams, and potential roles.

Sociology of emotions

The sociological study of emotions "articulates the links between cultural ideals, and...the way we wish we felt, the way we try to feel, the way we feel, the way we show what we feel, and the way we...make sense of what we feel" (Hochschild, 1987, p. 117). Historical approaches in the sociology of emotions have found that the distributions of specific emotions (such as grief, jealousy, and love) have varied with historical, cultural, and structural shifts (Thoits, 1987, p. 174). The qualities of these variations have been explored at the micro-level, often from a symbolic interactionist perspective. Symbolic interactionists who study the sociology of emotions argue that our feelings are tied not only to subjective experience, but that they exist as a result of our ability to be influenced by others and to respond to those influences. People actively interpret the reactions and behaviors of others to explain and define the significance of their own physiological states (Palmer, 1991). Thus, the subjective feelings that we have and express are labeled, supported, reflected, diminished, or denied by others, and we in turn alter our subjective feelings in reaction to the responses of others.

Arlie Hochschild (1983) has studied emotional labor in the workplace, but many of her concepts apply to the private sphere as well. Emotional labor refers to the acts that one must perform to induce or suppress one's own feeling in order to sustain the outward appearance that will elicit desired responses and assessments from others (Hochschild, 1983, p. 7). Emotional labor is the handling or working up of one's own emotion in order to achieve, in the Marxist sense, exchange value. Some examples of exchange value that might accrue to "properly" grieving parents could include being perceived as courageous in the face of difficulty, gaining social status by acting sensibly, being (ap)praised as strong because one is "getting on with one's life." According to Hochschild, feelings are governed by feeling rules or commonly held understandings of what is owed and owing in emotional interaction. As Hochschild (1983) states, "we can offend against a feeling rule when we grieve too much or too little" (p. 64).

Parents whose loss is not social and whose grief is hence not seen as legitimate often find themselves offending against commonly held feeling rules. Parents are continually told how they should and should not feel, and yet those feeling rules come into harsh juxtaposition with their actual emotions. Hochschild (1983) states that actors engage in emotional labor to manage their outward expression of feeling and perform emotion work to actively manage their subjective feelings as well. This manipulation of our own feelings is guided by latent feeling rules, rules which are internalized and which tell us what we "should" feel and what we are entitled to feel. Parental emotion work, thus, becomes a rearranging of parents' subjective experiences so that they line up with publicly-held and privately internalized versions of what bereaved parents "should" and "should not" feel. The burden of this additional emotion work makes perinatal grief particularly poignant.

Related to the social construction of grief is the concept of disenfranchised grief, where an individual experiences a subjective sense of loss "but does not have a socially recognized right, role, or capacity to grieve" (Doka,

1987). According to Doka, society has fairly consensual grieving rules that set out who, when, where, how, how long, and for whom people should grieve. He outlines three reasons why grief is disenfranchised: because the relationship is not recognized (as in the case of lovers and mistresses of deceased persons); because the loss is not recognized (as in the case of secret losses such as adopting out a child or socially insignificant losses such as a pregnancy loss); and finally, because the griever is not recognized (as in the case of mentally handicapped people who may be perceived to be incapable of understanding the loss) (Doka, 1989). Perinatal grief becomes disenfranchised primarily because the loss is not recognized or socially significant.

According to Doka, disenfranchised grief is paradoxical. Although the purpose of disenfranchising another's grief is to negate and delegitimate grief feelings, the circumstances of disenfranchisement actually complicate and intensify feelings of grief. Feelings of loss become compounded by feelings of shame, isolation, and alienation from traditional sources of solace, such as planning and attending funeral rituals, access to religious rites such as baptisms, "working through" grief publicly with family members, and being entitled to bereavement leave or insurance benefits (Doka, 1987).

Grief literature

The above discussion sheds some light on personal beliefs and attitudes of parents that might make perinatal grieving difficult, and it begins to paint a picture of how social and public responses might further add to difficulties in grieving. A third aspect particular to perinatal loss is the actual nature of death. I am arguing that perinatal death fulfills all the attributes of trauma. Tedeschi and Calhoun (1995, pp. 16–18) describe trauma as events

- that are sudden and unexpected;
- over which individuals perceive they have no control;
- that are out of the ordinary;
- that create long-lasting problems;
- that sufferers cannot blame someone else for; and
- that occur at critical junctures in the life cycle of victims.

Tedeschi and Calhoun (1995) describe extraordinarily difficult life crises as trauma. First, trauma occurs when the event itself is a shock, occurring suddenly and unexpectedly. The death of a child in pregnancy or at term is indeed sudden and unexpected. Both as individuals and as a society we rarely expect infants to die; in fact, we expect to know our children until we ourselves die. A second element of trauma is the perceived lack of control that sufferers have over the traumatic event. When I recall the moment my amniotic sac broke far too early in pregnancy, I liken it to that instant at the top of the first downhill run of a roller coaster; I felt a horrible calm, yet I knew that soon things would start running away from me, and no matter how much I willed it to be different, I was never going to be able to get off that ride.

Third, trauma occurs when an event is out of the ordinary, meaning that victims are not able to anticipate it or know how to respond to it. Surely the loss of an infant is perceived to be out of the ordinary—although as many as 20–30% of all pregnancies result in miscarriage, ectopic pregnancy, premature delivery, or stillbirth, "a veil of silence surrounds pregnancy loss in our culture" (Layne, 1990), making the event seem extraordinary to those who suffer through it. The promise of medicine, too, contributes to expectations of a healthy, living child as an ordinary outcome of pregnancy. The net result is that parents are not led to expect the death of a baby and are certainly not prepared to deal with it when it does happen.

A fourth aspect of trauma is the degree to which it creates long-lasting problems or the degree of irreversibility involved in the loss. The death of a child is indeed irreversible, and although some parents do go on to subsequent pregnancies, the dead child is never truly "replaced."

The fifth factor Tedeschi and Calhoun cite in trauma is blame. Paradoxically, they claim that people who blame others for their losses are likely to have more problems resolving their grief than those who blame themselves. Their explanation is counterintuitive; however, the ability to accept responsibility also means that one believes one can change future outcomes or avoid further trauma. Parents who "do everything right" yet still lose their children experience profound feelings of helplessness and hopelessness.

Finally, the point in the life cycle at which a crisis occurs is an element in trauma. Tedeschi and Calhoun claim events that occur once an identity is well-established and that threaten that sense of identity can be deeply traumatic. Thus, a person whose identity is invested in being whole, healthy, and "normal" may experience the inability to carry a baby to term as highly threatening to their sense of self. My experience of myself as nurturing and self-reliant, for example, came into question when I came up against pregnancy loss. Likewise, a woman who is highly invested in traditional expectations of being a mother may find the loss of that possibility extremely threatening to her identity.

Tedeschi and Calhoun (1995) do not directly define trauma in terms of how terrible it is to experience, although they do refer to unwanted, unbidden images intruding into the minds of people who have experienced trauma and to numbness and shock as responses to trauma. Perhaps they neglect to cite the horror of the event as a factor because their definition of trauma victims includes survivors of those involved in the actual events, including, for example, family members of people who have been murdered. In their discussions, the trauma victims may not have witnessed the events. In the case of perinatal loss, however, distance is not possible. Women who bear dead children not only witness the event, but are active participants in it. Thus, for women who bear a dead baby, and for the partners who attend them in the delivery room, there is an additional element of horror in the trauma of perinatal loss.

Complicated mourning

It is apparent that mourners' attitudes and beliefs about themselves and their dead babies, social practices and norms surrounding perinatal death, and the actual nature of the death as a traumatic event all converge to form a picture of perinatal death as a profound and extraordinarily painful life event. Thus, although the loss is a small one—a not-yet-born infant who has had little or no apparent impact beyond the changing of a mother's dress size or the wallpapering of a nursery—the hole such a small loss leaves behind is enormous. Traditionally, when a discrepancy exists between the nature of a loss and the profundity of its grief, this discrepancy has been described as "inexplicable" or "pathological" grief (Fowlkes, 1991, p. 529). Fowlkes (1991) goes on to say that "what we might be inclined to think of as melancholia or pathological grief may be a mourner's response to loss that relevant onlookers do not know so well" (p. 529). In other words, the grief reaction is not pathological; rather, it only seems so because outsiders fail to truly understand the magnitude of what has been lost. Fowlkes (1991) states that in situations where a loss is not understood by others, the mourner finds him/herself at odds with his/her social milieu and is forced to rely solely on her/his own resources to negotiate her/his grief resolution, resulting in intensified and complicated mourning (p. 533).

Complicated mourning, according to Therese Rando (1992), occurs when "taking into consideration the amount of time since the death, there is a compromise, distortion or failure of one or more of the six 'R' processes of mourning that are normally necessary to the healthy accommodation of any loss" (p. 45). In Rando's model, as in Fowlkes' discussion above, the process of grieving in complicated mourning is no different than the process of grieving in "regular" mourning. The difference between "normal" and "complicated" mourning rests in how grievers are able to work through standard processes of grief. Mourning is not complicated because of something inherently pathological within the griever; rather, people suffer complicated mourning because of the challenges outside themselves that they face in accomplishing the six "R's" of mourning. According to Rando (1992), the six "R" processes necessary for healthy accommodation of loss require that mourners:

1. recognize, acknowledge and understand the death as having occurred;
2. react to the separation by feeling the pain and giving some form of expression to both the primary loss and losses that are secondary to the death;
3. recollect and reexperience the deceased and the lost relationship, reviewing and remembering realistically;
4. relinquish old attachments to the deceased and to one's previous assumptive world;
5. readjust and move adaptively into the new world without forgetting the old by developing a new relationship with the deceased, with one's previous assumptions and with one's new identity; and
6. reinvest in life. (p. 45)

In light of the intrapsychic and social forces that act upon grieving parents and of the traumatic nature of the death itself, I believe that negotiating each of these six 'R' processes is bound to be difficult for parents who have lost a child to perinatal death. Thus, I will use Rando's model of complicated mourning to organize my analysis of parental narratives of loss and grief.

Rando (1993) describes grief as "the process of experiencing the psychological, behavioral, social and physical reactions to the perception of loss" (p. 22). Grief, then, is intrinsic to the individual and encompasses the person's own feelings about the loss, their physical responses to the loss, their wish to undo it, and the personal actions that these feelings, wishes and responses elicit. Charmaz (1980) states that grief is "the subjective, emotional response to the death of the significant other" (p. 280). Mourning, on the other hand, is "the process through which grief is faced and ultimately resolved or altered over time" (Charmaz, 1980, p. 280). To Rando (1993), mourning includes not only the public display of grief, but it concerns itself with the intrapsychic and interpersonal processes that act to resolve the grief (p. 23).

In my discussion, I will use the term grief to refer to what the bereaved person feels in direct reaction to the loss. I will use the term mourning to discuss what the bereaved person does both internally and in interaction over the long term in order to resolve their grief.

Chapter 2
How Perinatal Loss is Experienced

Informed by my literature review and my personal experience, I conducted interviews with 25 parents who have experienced perinatal loss. The story that follows is no one particular person's story; rather, it represents commonalities in how parents in my study lived through perinatal loss.

Before beginning with parents' stories, however, it is necessary to say a word about the language of perinatal loss. In professional language related to perinatal death, in the language used in the literature, in the language used by parent support groups, and in the language of individual parents themselves, there is some ambiguity about how to name perinatal death. Lay language used to describe perinatal death includes "miscarriage" (referring to infant loss occurring within the first trimester), "pregnancy loss" (infant loss during later pregnancy), "stillbirth" (infant loss during birth), and "death" (losses that occur after the infant's birth). Legal definitions of death, often related to parental leave, death benefits and insurance coverage, are often solely related to infants who have lived for a minimum period of time. Medical definitions relate to infant viability, with infant losses that occur prior to 20 weeks being referred to as "fetal wastage" or "spontaneous abortion." However, for the parents I spoke with, regardless of the duration of the pregnancy or the number of losses or the opinions of doctors, employers, family members and significant others, the loss was experienced as a death, something to be mourned, something that left them forever changed. Thus, I choose consciously to use the term "perinatal death" or "perinatal loss" to describe the losses of all the infants in this study who died before, during, or shortly following birth. A more thorough description of the infants and their parents whose stories are represented in this book can be found in Appendix A.

BEFORE THE LOSS—IGNORANCE IS NOT ALWAYS BLISS

Men and women rarely knew much about perinatal loss before they encountered it themselves. They never discussed the topic in their doctor visits, they did not hear it in their prenatal classes, and if they knew of it through friends or family, their understanding was that is was an unlikely event that would never affect them. One woman, a physician, said,

> I knew that it happened. I didn't realize how common it was....I hadn't processed it. I knew it happened, but I didn't think it was gonna happen to me. And I thought if it was going to happen it would happen within those first 3 months, so by the time I'd gotten past twelve weeks, I thought I was home and dry.

A common theme in discussing preparedness for pregnancy loss was that people knew the first 3 months are a dangerous time and were unprepared when problems arose after that period. Before their own losses, participants shared common beliefs about perinatal loss: that is, such events occur early in pregnancy; they are due to deformity or lack of viability in the infant; biological or moral maternal defects, such as smoking, drinking, poor diet, and excess worry or ambivalence contribute to perinatal loss; and ultimately, if babies do die, it is for a "good" reason. As one woman said, "I knew people that had miscarriages, but I also believed that it was God's way of dealing with a baby that couldn't live." Their beliefs, although reflecting commonly held notions about perinatal loss, often stood in opposition to the reality of their children's deaths—perinatal death often occurs for no apparent reason. The babies who died in this study were seemingly perfect, there were rarely maternal diagnoses to account for the deaths, and most women stated they were careful about their physical and mental health while pregnant.

Parents not only underestimated the physical possibility of perinatal loss, but they also failed to understand how emotionally devastating such a loss might be. Even those whose training was in nursing or medicine had little experience with parental bereavement. One woman, in discussing her nursing school experience on an obstetrics ward, said,

> Ah, there had been a discussion on an intellection level about—they call it "complications of pregnancy." But that was on an intellectual,

not an emotional level. In Obstetrics we were not allowed to work on any of those more emotional issues—that was more for the staff nurses and doctors to handle.

The lack of knowledge that parents have about both the physical and emotional aspects of perinatal loss reflects a general lack of discussion in society; the topic is kept quiet. Yet, as several people noted, once they had suffered a pregnancy loss, they were frequently approached by friends and acquaintances who disclosed their own stories of loss. Several parents reported hearing for the first time about mothers and grandmothers who had perinatal losses only after they had experienced their own loss. Others were approached by friends, family members, and even strangers. As one woman explains:

Oh, they came out of the woodwork afterwards! My mother kept hearing stories about this cousin's friend, and this aunt's friend, and this—oh, I was just hearing story after story. Why couldn't I hear about this before?

Apparently, the silence surrounding perinatal loss does not reflect the frequency with which it occurs.

When asked to speculate why silence surrounds the subject, one woman ventured, "I think it's because we don't want to scare anyone, particularly anyone who is pregnant." Most participants felt that discussing the possibility of pregnancy loss with pregnant parents is inappropriate because "in most situations the baby is born fine and if they talk about it a lot then it gives it too much emphasis that this can happen, and that could make things more difficult." Nonetheless, parents also acknowledged that if they had been prepared for some of the experiences and feelings they ultimately did encounter they might not have felt so alone, and their journey might have been easier. As one woman noted, "I really don't think you should protect people. People should be treated like adults, and if there is information that might help them in some way, they should have it."

During the loss—Numbness and disbelief

People in this study experienced their actual losses in a variety of ways. For some parents, the pregnancy of their children was normal and full-term, with no indications that anything was amiss until the very last instant. For a few, the pregnancies finally ended after lengthy problems of intrauterine bleeding, cramping and threatened premature labor. For still others, everything seemed to be going well until premature labor began. Some parents were forced to make the choice to discontinue measures to save the pregnancy, and others were swept up in a maelstrom of activity with little or no say in how matters unfolded. Regardless of the particulars of the actual loss, parents spoke of common emotional experiences during their children's deaths.

Parents talked about numbness and a feeling of shock. More often than not, these parents knew before the actual deaths that their infants would not live. For example, mothers whose amniotic sacs had ruptured, although technically still pregnant, often were compelled to decide to induce labor, knowing that such labor would mean the death of their babies. Mothers whose babies had died in utero also knew that to deliver would mean to deliver a dead child. They held vain hopes that something magical would intervene, that some malfunction in the ultrasound machine would be discovered, that the heartbeat would be found again, or that broken membranes would heal. Parents spoke of waiting for their babies to die but not yet feeling grief. Although they knew intellectually that their children were dead or would die soon, the experiential knowledge of the death's meaning only came later. One woman put it well:

> I mean, the nurses even said to me—they knew she—the baby—was dead—and it was like 24 hours before I had her, and that whole time they talked to me about how I was gonna feel, and I didn't believe them. My response was, "Well, these things happen. I have to have the baby now, and I have to get on with my life."

For this woman, as for many others in the study, the initial understanding of their loss was based on common cultural beliefs about perinatal loss. The only framework they had for the experience was that this was a small thing, to be gotten through so they could move on with their lives. It was only later that they began to understand their loss. The initial lack of understanding often contributed to decisions that were later regretted. Parents, failing to understand what they were about to lose, also failed to take advantage of opportunities to hold their babies and say goodbye, to request autopsies, to arrange funerals, or to demand death certificates.

Disbelief was a common reaction. Women often described ignoring physical symptoms, such as fetal nonmovement or leaking amniotic fluid. Often, when they did have suspicions, these were minimized or ignored by medical personnel, and sometimes parents grasped at medical assurances because they so desperately wanted to believe that nothing was wrong with their babies.

Even when knowledge of the loss exists on an intellectual level, it is hard to give up hope. One woman said she refused to push in the delivery room. Her baby was already dead, and to her, pushing meant giving in. Not pushing became a way for her to exercise some control over a situation that was clearly running away from her. Another woman spoke of her ambivalence, referring to the supreme injustice of "giving death"—to have the act of birthing be simultaneously the act of killing. A woman whose child was too premature to be expected to survive through labor said, "The worst thing was still feeling the baby kick and knowing that it was alive and that I'd killed it. 'Cause that's what it felt like—to deliver her was to kill her."

Even those women who had experienced multiple losses described a sense of disbelief—"this can't be happening to me again." Some of these women spoke of *déjà vu,* of knowing exactly what was going to happen in the next hours, months and years, and how much worse that knowledge made things. They did not hold out those same fierce hopes of a miracle, yet they still spoke of being numb despite knowing what was to come. While the actual birth occurred, there was detachment, a not-yet-grief for a baby not-yet-dead.

For fathers, the sense of unreality and numbness is somewhat different. They, too, described not yet understanding the profundity of their loss. However, their primary focus was a common concern for their wives' health and mental well-being. They clearly perceived their role as a supportive one and their feelings as secondary to their wives' feelings. This perception was upheld by hospital experiences. Fathers were often left unattended in the delivery room, forgotten while more pressing medical events unfolded. Feelings of helplessness and unimportance were common. As one man said,

> Basically, I think they just forgot me in all the rush and excitement. Then, once the baby was finally out, they still had my wife to attend to. They handed him to me, and I just kind of wandered off to another room and held him until he died. I didn't know what to do with him after that.

What clearer message about priorities could be given? A man and an unsavable baby are left to their own devices, while the more "serious" drama of the mother's struggle for life unfolds.

After the Loss—A Whole New Understanding

Once the babies are delivered and the mothers' conditions are stabilized, parents have to come to terms with the world beyond the delivery room. Family members and friends have to be told. Surviving children have to be dealt with and taken care of. Workplaces have to be notified. But first, parents have to deal with their babies. In the past, babies were often whisked away, and parents who wished to see and hold their babies were often denied that right. Things do seem to have improved over the past years as far as the medical response to miscarriage and stillbirth are concerned, although there are differences between hospitals (and between cities). Parents' hospital experiences, even in the same hospitals, were quite varied. One woman, whose loss occurred over a weekend, received no photos or footprints. She had no contact with a social worker or pastor. Her visit with her baby was extremely brief and was curtailed abruptly. She was kept on a maternity floor following her child's stillbirth and listened to women delivering healthy babies for several hours after her loss. Finally, her husband was told to leave because visiting hours were over, and no exceptions could be made. She learned subsequently that her experience had occurred because of staff shortages, but her opportunities to retrieve those moments were lost forever.

There are no commonly held norms for grieving a dead baby, and these parents only later understood that they had needed more direction from caregivers because they simply had no idea what to do, what to consider, and what they might regret later. This lack of direction from caregivers was reinforced by how little parents knew about loss and death before their babies died and how little information is available generally on how to acknowledge and honor the death of a preterm or stillborn child.

Ideally, hospitals do provide photographs and footprints; however, they rarely tell parents what to do, making suggestions only. Although this nondirective approach is likely well-intended, most parents wished someone had been there "to show me how to do it properly." One woman describes how being pushed helped her:

> And when she was born I didn't want to see her. And they actually kind of bullied me into it. They wrapped her up and put her in my arms, then they took her away and gave her a bath and brought her back. And sort of bullied us into a position to spend time with her. Which was an excellent thing. It really was. It was just the best thing, because it put closure on it.

In this couple's case, although they might not have appreciated it at the time, being forced to say goodbye came to be one of the more positive memories they could share.

Suggesting rituals as an option rather than as an expectation amounts to a tacit message that this is merely a gesture for a make-believe loss. For example, if a husband dies, hospitals do not ask wives if they would like a funeral or if they would prefer the hospital to dispose of the remains; these questions are, however, asked of parents who experience the death of an infant. Death certificates are very frequently not provided by the hospital staff; they are mentioned in passing, and parents are given the "option" of not having one. This option is usually presented as something that will save parents a few dollars and a lot of hassle. In reality, several parents expressed regrets that they did not have death certificates for their children. In our culture, certificates can confer "legitimacy"; not issuing a certificate implies perinatal death is not legitimate.

For most parents, pregnancy is not a time of preparing for death. Parents do not take out life insurance policies for their children until after they are born, nor do they think to put aside enough money to buy a nice cemetery plot and headstone. Many new parents have just finished planning and executing a wedding and may be thinking of how to throw a christening party, but they have probably given little thought to what type of funeral they might want for their child. Parents do not know what gestures might be appropriate to commemorate the passing of a baby who is expected to live, not die. Yet these are precisely the types of decisions that parents were required to make. Many expressed a wish that they could have had more guidance and more time to make decisions about funerals, burial plots, autopsies, death certificates, whether or not to hold their babies, how long to hold their babies and what mementoes they might wish to have.

Even when parents did have specific ideas about how to commemorate their loss, they described struggling to create the rituals they wished to observe. Funeral directors were reluctant to allow parents to hold or dress babies, especially if an autopsy had been performed. Nursing staff were often reluctant to leave babies with parents "too long," being concerned with aesthetics and hygiene. Parents spoke of asking to take their babies home before funerals and being refused, of coming back to hospitals a day or two after the death in hopes of seeing their babies one last time only to find they were too late. Sometimes, parents were unsure what happened to their babies afterward and were afraid to find out, so they never enquired.

Outside of the medical community, parents ran into resistance from others in commemorating their loss. Not all parents had funerals or memorial services, but those who did frequently attended those rituals alone. Many parents discussed the pain of having family members or friends not come to the funeral. People often failed to send cards or flowers, again treating the loss as a nonevent. Sometimes, mothers or close relatives who had planned to come out to "help with the baby" ended up cancelling their visit "because you won't be needing me anymore." For others, grandparents did not arrive because there were other situations that were more pressing—a sister who had a viable newborn needed more help, or a relative who was ill needed tending. On the other hand, some parents were pleasantly surprised by unexpected support, often from unanticipated quarters. Neighbors and acquaintances who had previously been merely polite often came to the fore, frequently because they had their own losses. There is a solidarity in shared experience.

ALIENATION

Parents likened the time following their losses to adolescence; they felt misunderstood, alienated from others, alienated from themselves. Those who formerly saw themselves as outgoing, caring people found themselves unable to take joy in the pregnancies of friends or to tolerate seeing children the same age as their own child would be. Friends became distanced not simply because they failed to support parents (although that happened, too), but because the parents themselves were no longer carefree and fun-loving people, having become almost too sad to be part of life.

In the workplace, women were often refused time off from work or did not have their loss acknowledged. At best, companies sent a bouquet of flowers. One woman returned to work the day after her loss and was confronted by her boss who said, "You should have told me you were thinking of getting pregnant, and now *this*." When this woman became pregnant and lost her baby a second time, she never returned to work. Another woman was refused maternity leave, despite being entitled to it. The employer told her there would have been no problem in getting maternity leave "if the baby had lived" but failed to see the need for time off without a baby to care for. Her physician signed for extended sick leave, but upon her return to the job, she lost her seniority. She left the job 6 months later. Coworkers as well as employers were clear in their desire to see women move on and "get back to normal," often refusing to listen to women's stories or avoiding them altogether.

For men, the workplace was even less accommodating. Most men got no time off from work. One man, who works with his father in a family business, had to risk a rift in the family in order to take the time off that he, wisely, felt he needed. His father felt that a speedy return to work would be "the best remedy" for dealing with his sorrow. The son's willingness to fight for what he felt he needed was not perceived as a strength; he ultimately ended up having to deal with the secondary burden of being thought "soft" by his father/boss.

Unfortunately, the ability to resist social pressure and stand up for one's needs is difficult for parents because their grief is frequently debilitating. As one woman said, "I needed pampering. I just needed to be told what to do." Parents were simply unable to advocate for themselves, often feeling bullied into returning to work before they were ready to or only realizing that they had returned to work too soon once they had forfeited the right to maternity benefits.

Women felt particularly alienated by the way others seemed to expect them to "get on with life." Women who felt their marital relationships were warm, open and communicative found themselves unable to share their grief with their partners. Husbands were frequently described as "getting over it much sooner than I did," "grieving differently," and being "less devastated than me."

Thus, for women, lovers and husbands were also sources of alienation. Women often spoke of being alone late at night, their partners sleeping beside them, as they went over things again and again. Although most of the participants were still with their partners, they spoke of "rough periods" in their marriage, which occurred when each grieved in ways incomprehensible to the other.

For fathers, there was a silent, internal grief. They described feeling their role was to take care of their wives rather than indulge in their own sorrow. For mothers, the need to talk, to process their experience with their partners was often not satisfied. Women spoke of feeling that their partners became weary of discussing the loss long before they were able to let it go. They felt they were dwelling on things too long; at the same time, they were concerned that their partners were not dealing adequately with their own grief. For both parents, the pressures of daily living—running a household, making a living, caring for surviving children, "acting normal" with friends and family—created additional burdens.

Friends and family members failed to understand the profundity of parents' pain. The interviews are replete with anecdotes of insensitive and foolish efforts to comfort or minimize parents' feelings. Parents were told that "they could always have another," "it was God's way of doing things," "these things happen for a reason," and "at least you have one living child." Men were told to "be strong for your wife—she needs you now," implying that men have no need of their own to grieve. These comments failed miserably to provide comfort. The one thing parents, particularly mothers, did want, that is, to be heard, seemed to be impossible to get. Above all, others were unwilling or unable to sit with these parents and hear their pain. When asked why they participated in this project, interviewees expressed basically one thought: I wanted to be able to tell my story so that it might help some other parent to feel less alone.

To tell one's story is a profound and persistent need. All of the women I spoke with said they wanted to talk about their losses in multiple settings;

but instead of being permitted to discuss their losses—in effect, to debrief—they encountered seeming disinterest or discomfort whenever the topic came up. Mothers of dead babies feel themselves to be pariahs; they are not permitted to speak about their loss. There is a Kafka-esque quality to this experience: they talk, and no one hears; they approach, and the world avoids. Often, they are not even permitted to contribute to discussions about motherhood and pregnancy. As one woman said,

> At some level, I am not allowed to talk about my pregnancy—like, when others are talking about morning sickness, there's a decided change in the conversation if I should bring my pregnancy experiences up. Because my pregnancy doesn't belong in a conversation with other women's pregnancies.

Not only is open discussion of the experience of perinatal loss treated as abnormal, but for women, their actual womanhood is abnormal. Because of their particular experiences, they are excluded from the normal rituals of womanhood, such as discussing one's pregnancy or delivery; they are no longer part of the club.

FEAR

Late-night loneliness is a leitmotif; women report waking up feeling kicks from babies no longer there, hearing cries from babies who never lived. Women commonly responded with fear to these late-night wakenings: as their partners slept in seeming peace, they feared they were losing their minds. Because their grieving took place in silence and isolation, they wondered whether or not it was appropriate. It certainly felt authentic, but with all the pressures to move on and stop "obsessing," women experienced a real fear that their emotions were out of control and that they were out of control as well.

Another fear people experience results from ignorance. Parents reported knowing very little about birthing and even less about giving birth to babies who do not survive. The public conception that such deaths are for the best implies that the infant is perhaps deformed or subnormal. Several parents mentioned refusing to see their babies because they feared what the baby would look like. All expressed regrets over this choice; because of fear, they lost their opportunity to say good-bye. Although hospital staff did offer them the option of looking at their babies, they were unable to take advantage of the choice. Their fears were not spoken out loud (they were hesitant to look foolish), so nursing or medical practitioners were not called upon to assure them that their babies were not "freaks." The need for parents to be guided through this process was expressed repeatedly. The fear of the unknown and the fear of appearing foolish left parents unable to ask for the guidance they needed most.

Following the birth experience, there was also a fear that one might literally go mad from grief. One woman vividly described her sense that it was only her mother's intervention that kept her from "going over the edge and never coming back." Facing the darkness and learning how precarious sanity can be leaves one knowing that one's own sanity cannot necessarily be relied upon. The world becomes a scarier place without such basic assumptions.

Also, women who experience an infant death fear they will never produce healthy children. Subsequent pregnancies are fraught with misgivings and anxieties. The innocence of a trouble-free pregnancy is never to be regained. Women spoke of being unable to decide to have subsequent children. They often were relieved to "find" themselves pregnant (thus no longer needing to decide), yet they felt as though they had stepped in front of a train when they became pregnant. Would the horror recur? One of my respondents was 7 months pregnant at the time of our interview. She had not yet purchased any baby items and referred consistently to "if" we have the baby rather than "when." Her husband, in a separate interview, said,

I'm just not willing to get excited about this. I don't even think I will be able to afterwards. I just think it'll take a long time before I can really let myself believe we are going to have a kid.

Parents also worry about their surviving children. They have learned that life is not reliable, and they describe poignantly the tension between their overprotective parenting and their desire not to stifle their children. These parents describe themselves as much more protective and concerned with their other children than before the loss. Their fears extend to partners as well. One woman expressed several times during the interview how since the loss she worries about her husband crossing the C-train track twice each day on his commute to work. For her, the world has become a dangerous and unpredictable place.

SORROW

The sorrow parents feel is overwhelming. Parents have lost much more than a child. They have lost innocence. Their belief that the world is a safe place, that they themselves are stable, happy people, that life is predictable is shattered; none of these fundamentals can be counted on. Parents know that they will never be the young, carefree people they were before the loss. They describe a poignancy in parenting their surviving children, in knowing how fleeting life is and how these children, too, will leave them someday.

There is sorrow at not having fully said goodbye, of not having fully parented. Parents were often so numb at the time that they did not fully acknowledge their babies. They wish they had spent more time with them, had created more mementoes, had gone ahead with a funeral service. The women in this study wished they had been better at pregnancy, had been less (or more) emotionally invested in the pregnancy, had eaten better (or less), had not waited so long to become pregnant, had rested (or exercised) more, or had followed (or ignored) advice.

The women I spoke with felt they had let others down: that is, they felt they had failed their babies, their husbands, their surviving children, and their parents. One woman was very upset when describing how she felt she had let her father down, how she had hoped to give him his first grandson, and how deeply unsettling it had been to see him break down and cry—something she had never seen before, and something for which she felt responsible. One woman spoke of how inadequate she feels when her daughter wishes aloud for a sister or brother; not only does she regret disappointing her child, but it stirs up her own feelings of sorrow and loss. She questions, too, what the impact is on this child: what does she think about pregnancy, having seen her mother go to the hospital twice only to lose the baby? There is a sense that she feels responsible not only for her own sorrow, but for her daughter's lost innocence as well.

Women spoke of letting their partners down, of not being able to give them children: "That's what women do, isn't it—have babies?" Although most stated their husbands had been supportive, they still regretted not being able to provide their partners with a child. Conversely, men felt they had let their partners down by trying too hard, too soon, to act as though life were going to carry on normally. The men I spoke with were perhaps an extraordinary lot for even being willing to talk to me. Their awareness that things could have been done differently often came through a lot of marital discussion, sometimes augmented by support-group education or therapy sessions. They had *learned* that their initial responses were regrettable.

Other regrets extended to friends and family members. Friendships with others had changed—they felt distanced from former, frivolous friends and resented those who were able to have children without difficulty. Parents often avoided old friends whose children acted as painful reminders of what could have been.

GUILT

Women felt guilty about things they might have done differently: if only I had not been working so hard, I might not have lost the baby. Maybe I could have rested more; perhaps I was too tense. Maybe I did not want the baby enough; maybe I wanted it too much. Former reproductive choices also figure prominently. Women who had abortions or who had deferred child-bearing into their thirties felt an additional responsibility for their loss. Both parents wondered if the decisions they had made in the hospital were the best ones. Often, their lack of information left them feeling responsible for situations that were probably beyond their control. One man spoke of how he and his wife were called back to the hospital (in Toronto) to fully discuss the history of their son's death. They were debriefed at each stage of the infant's history on the difficult decisions they had been forced to make. This experience was a great help for them in resolving all of the "what if's" that often remain once the crisis is passed.

Women in our culture are trained to nurture and care for others, often before caring for themselves. Many women spoke of letting others down, of being a failure. Women spoke of how hard it was for husbands, children, and parents to have to go through this. One woman spoke of how painful it must have been for her mother to have to go through the experience because she, too, had a stillbirth many years earlier. Another described how difficult it had been for her husband because he had lost a child to Sudden Infant Death Syndrome (SIDS) in a previous marriage. Women accepted, even in this setting, that they were somehow responsible for the feelings of others, and this created an additional burden of guilt for them.

Conversely, men are taught in Western society that their role is to be instrumental. They should take charge of situations and take care of their families. Almost all of the women talked about how difficult it had been for their partners to have to watch them suffer and be unable to do anything to "fix" the situation. In most of the situations in this study, such expectations were virtually impossible. This inability to "make it right" left men feeling guilty and frustrated.

It seems traditional sex roles can cut both ways. Men feel guilt for not being able to control things or take care of their wives; women feel guilt for not being able to make everyone happy by producing a bouncing, healthy baby.

Guilt was evident long after the loss. Women felt guilty because they could not be happy for friends and family who subsequently had children. Some women spoke of feeling guilty because they were self-absorbed following the death, resulting in a neglect of their living children and partners. For many women, the need to be alone and to live through their grief meant taking time away from their normal roles of wife, mother, worker, community member, and friend. Even being sad can mean feeling guilty for women who feel it is their duty to serve the emotional needs of others and put their own needs last.

ANGER

There was a lot of anger in the parents' stories. They were angry at physicians who promised more than they could deliver or who were perceived as neglectful. One woman actually set out on a late-night sojourn with the intent of finding her physician and killing her. Although this is an extreme example of anger at the medical profession, there were others who felt the information and services they had received were inadequate. Parents complained of not being told enough, of not being prepared for what happened, of not being listened to when they first reported their concerns and misgivings. This lack of validation seemed particularly painful; women's preloss fears were often minimized, and on at least two occasions, the unwillingness of doctors to treat complaints seriously did appear to contribute to the pregnancy loss.

Parents were often dissatisfied with the level of information they received after the loss. They described being a focus of much interest and attention in the hospital as long as medical events were unfolding, but once the baby had died, they felt abandoned by medical and nursing staff. Few parents were given the kind of postloss care provided to the Toronto couple, where medical practitioners outlined the decisions made and assured them they had made the right ones. In fact, most parents were unable to receive any information about what had gone wrong, which resulted in additional questions about past events and tremendous uncertainty regarding future reproductive decisions. Autopsies, it seems, are rarely performed until a third perinatal loss has occurred. Understandably, not all parents are willing to go through such a loss three times before knowing what, if any, infant pathology may be a contributor to or cause of the death. According to Layne (1990, p. 70), perinatal pathology is the least developed branch of pathology. This lack of knowledge was reflected in the experience of these parents, who were told by medical personnel, both in words and through a a lack of medical investigation, that "these things just happen."

Parents also felt anger at their churches. Some wanted nothing to do with their priests or pastors, feeling betrayed by their faith. Some said that having a religious background raised more questions than it did answers. After all, these were good people who had followed their faith well. Why were they being punished? Well-meaning comments about this being God's will or God's way of preventing a freak of nature offered cold comfort.

Only one woman, a Buddhist, mentioned that she felt comforted by the comments of a Buddhist monk who told her how good it was that her daughter only needed 9 months to complete her journey. Even a woman who ultimately became a Minister described her feelings of anger at God; she felt that her anger at God was a pivotal step in her sense-making, and without that anger, she doubted she would have been able to find the peace she ultimately gained.

The anger parents feel towards God is born out of a sense of injustice. Likewise, women's feelings about abortion, choice, and childless couples arise from a sense of injustice. A physician described having to counsel a 15-year-old patient who was pregnant and wanted an abortion. The injustice of the situation left her sobbing and unable to see patients. People described subtle shifts in their attitudes towards abortion. Although none of them were adamant prolife advocates, they felt that abortion is often undertaken "too lightly" and that women should receive more counselling than they believe occurs. These parents have often gone to heroic measures to have a child, experiencing repeated loss, multiple surgeries, and enforced bedrest. For many of them, the idea that a woman could actually *choose* not to have children was perceived as an insult: that what they wanted so desperately could be so cavalierly discarded seemed an affront. For 2 participants, this feeling extended not only to women who have abortions, but included women who choose childlessness as a way of living.

As well as those who choose not to bear children, those who bear them easily are sources of resentment. One woman described her sister as a "baby-machine—she's only 90 pounds! I mean she doesn't look like a baby machine, but she manages to have babies so easily. It just isn't fair!" Although parents deny harboring any ill wishes against those who have children without difficulty, they did express resentment. There was an underlying sense that others are not necessarily deserving of the charmed lives they lead and that learning some of life's hard lessons might not be such a bad thing for them.

Parents felt angry at well-meaning friends and family members whose advice and consolation were often woefully inadequate or misplaced. A commonly reported response is to offer advice. Parents are often told how they should feel: you should be happy you have other kids; you should be relieved because there was probably something wrong with the baby; don't feel sad, you are young and can always have more. Often the advice offered is wrong, almost always it is inappropriate.

There was also anger at those who responded by not say anything at all; friends who never called, parents who never sent cards or stayed away from the funeral, coworkers who did not even notice that women were no longer pregnant. Men reported that they were seldom given direct support; they were asked, "How's your wife doing?" as though the loss had nothing to do with them.

Although women were careful to acknowledge the support they received from their husbands, they also felt isolated by and angry at the different ways their partners experienced grief. Women wanted to talk, to share, to work things through in conversation. Men seemed to retreat into silence and "life as usual" as a way of coping. Another contentious issue for wives was how husbands seemed to relinquish subsequent reproductive choices to the woman. Woman were told "it's your body—you decide," when what they really wished for was an open and honest discussion both about what had happened and what they, as a couple, ought to do about it.

Conversely, one woman's partner had a vasectomy shortly after their second loss. While acknowledging that the decision was probably the right one, she resented feeling forced to live with a decision in which she had not fully participated. Another woman wished to discuss the possibility of abortion while she was losing the baby. She had been bleeding for several weeks, did not want the pregnancy in the first place, and felt that the baby would probably not survive in any case. Her husband refused to discuss the option of abortion. These complaints are, in a sense, flip sides of the same coin. Whether women are left to be solely responsible for reproductive decisions, or whether the topic is simply not open for discussion, the real issue is that they wish to be part of a partnership in making those choices. What women long for is the opportunity to talk things through, regardless of the final outcome of that talk.

Even surviving children are potential sources of anger and resentment. Little children often need more attention and reassurance than usual when their mothers are in hospital or suffer emotionally. Children's neediness is often expressed in "acting out." One woman described being at home on limited bedrest following a threatened miscarriage and the tension between her and her 3-year-old daughter. Normally a compliant, happy child, this little girl had refused to sit on her mother's bed in the hospital, visiting instead with other mothers on the ward. Once the mother was home, but still not emotionally available to her daughter, the little girl demonstrated a lot of anger and opposition. One morning, while struggling to prepare her child for daycare, this woman became so angry and so frightened that she might harm her child that she left the child unattended while she drove her car around the block to "cool off ."

Many people expressed feelings of shame, defined in Webster's dictionary as "a painful emotion aroused by the recognition that one has failed to act in accordance with the standard which one accepts as good." In modern

Western society, parenting is defined as "good" (Veevers, 1980). One man described feeling "marked." Upon return to work, he felt ashamed to face his coworkers, embarrassed by what had happened to him. Several people described being pregnant at the same time as other couples in their cohorts and avoiding those people when they had successful pregnancies. Women often discussed the macha nature of modern mothering; there are imperatives to deliver naturally, avoid anesthetics or medication during delivery, not require an episiotomy or C-Section, breastfeed blissfully, use nondisposable diapers, buy educational and developmentally appropriate toys, begin reading and basic literacy skills with children almost at birth, and look like a super model while doing so! These women are painfully aware of being "a failure" because "if you're a woman you can have babies, and if you can't have babies, I mean, that makes you less of a woman."

Because of the poor response and support parents receive from their intimates, they soon learn not to be open about their losses. One woman, in describing her late-night emotional wakenings, said, "I sort of kept it secret from my husband because he just didn't want to deal with me anymore." Woman were particularly concerned that they were grieving too long because their sense was that for everyone else this was a nonevent, something to be moved through and put away. Women do put the grief away but in the sense of locking it up in a drawer or placing it in a dark corner. The grief and the pain are there, but the emotions become shameful, something to be hidden. One of the women who responded to my call for information suffered a stillbirth in 1957. Only with the death of a subsequent child 23 years later did she come to say, "I realized with my son's death that I had not permitted myself to properly grieve my infant daughter."

CREATING RITUAL

Family and friends often failed to acknowledge the loss immediately or in the long run. Family members expressed dismay at seeing photos of dead babies displayed prominently in parents' homes. Anniversary dates of children's births/deaths were remembered only by mothers—hardly ever by grandparents and frequently not even by fathers.

Despite public denial, parents managed to honor their lost infants, although they often had little more than a packet of sympathy cards to commemorate their loss. At all of the interviews, women showed me their little packages: some containing the odd greeting card, some with photos and tiny footprints, some with an ultrasound picture. Women will look at these mementoes to observe anniversary dates, or simply, as one woman put it, "when I need that depth of emotion, to feel that it's real." Occasionally, these mementoes are displayed openly; more often, they are stored in drawers and closets, secret yet powerful. Interestingly, none of the men who were interviewed shared such mementoes with me.

Parents often spoke regretfully about not having done more to commemorate their children. Parents, although offered the option of having a funeral, often do not realize at the time how much that might mean to them in the future. Money, too, is often a factor in parents' regrets. Several of the parents interviewed had a funeral but years later had not been able to find the money for a headstone.

Likewise, parents wish they had spent more time, taken photos, written some sort of a baby book for their lost babies. It is as though by doing these things they might be able to make these babies more real, to keep their presence active. Particularly because these deaths go unacknowledged and the losses go unmourned, there is an urgency for parents to act as "keepers of the flame"; often they are solely responsible for keeping the memories alive. One woman, the mother of 9 first-trimester babies, had no remains, no photos, no death certificates, no cards, no mementoes. When asked about ritual, she poignantly described the ring she wore: a family ring, the 4 colored stones of the ring represented her, her husband and their two living children. They surrounded a large diamond. The diamond was for the babies, symbolizing the profound impact those brief lives had made on her own life.

For some, this use of talismans is a way of bringing the baby home. One woman described the presence of her child in the home. Six months after her death, the baby's picture sits on the mother's bedside table, booties and wristband next to it. The baby's room remains as it did before, with crib and stuffed toys still there. In a sense, the room had become something of a shrine. People ask her when the crib will be put away, expecting her to get rid of a painful reminder, but she described keeping the room intact as a way to keep her baby close to her in spirit at least.

Although several parents had their babies cremated, only one of these had actually placed the baby in a gravesite. The remainder kept the baby's remains in an urn at home. Accounts for this varied. Some women claimed their families were not yet settled enough in one place, and once they were in a permanent home, arrangements would be made to put the baby somewhere close to home. Others were ambivalent about letting the remains go; they claimed either not to see it as important enough to warrant the effort or said they preferred to keep the ashes with them. The general theme, however, seemed to be one of wanting to keep the baby close and protected, in a figurative if not a literal sense.

Another way women seemed to symbolize their pregnancies and their motherhood was through their body size. Several of the women interviewed were overweight, and most of them spontaneously said that they had been unable to shed 20–30 pounds since their loss. The weight gain recommended for pregnancy by physicians is 25 pounds. Orbach (1978, p. 57), in her discussion of fat, says that excess weight acts symbolically as a way for mourners to carry the dead person with them. One could easily infer that the weight gain is a way for women to maintain the illusion that they are still pregnant or to acknowledge physically that they have indeed been pregnant. For these women, looking pregnant may act to support their self-concept as maternal and nurturing women. Unfortunately, this interpretation was not clearly supported by women's passing comments, and indeed, many mothers of surviving babies complain abut losing their previous body shape and size once they have been pregnant.

RITES OF PASSAGE

The literature speaks of miscarriage as an incomplete rite of passage (Layne, 1990). In Western culture, becoming a full adult is accomplished by bearing children (Veevers, 1988). Thus, miscarriage can act to abort not only the baby, but it also aborts the process of becoming complete adults (Reinharz, 1988). I believe, however, that parents do accomplish rites of passage through their experience of loss.

Rites of passage are often conceived as a means of achieving membership in a group. One woman spoke hauntingly of the moment she was told her daughter was dead:

I screamed, and in that scream I felt a clear, universal connection to every woman throughout time who ever lost a child through famine, through war, through illness, through plague, through birth.

This woman achieved membership in universal womanhood quite literally. Other women spoke of the experience as a "coming of age," during which their relationships with their mothers underwent profound shifts. One refused to allow her mother into the delivery room as she felt her mother would have tried to tell her what to do; this became a declaration of independence for her. Another spoke of coming into conflict with her mother over some of the rituals she chose to observe following the death of her daughter. Her mother found them uncomfortable, and for the daughter, they became a way of asserting her right to make decisions for herself, reportedly for the first time in her life. Another spoke of finally receiving comfort and care from social workers and nursing staff and realizing that the mothering she had received had been inadequate. This new understanding of what nurturing should be led her to reframe her relationship with her mother on a more equitable basis.

Without necessarily conceptualizing their loss as a rite of passage, all of the participants in this study acknowledged that their experiences had left them profoundly changed. All of the parents spoke of being older, wiser, less innocent than their former selves. One spoke of merely having "played house" before, of not having any idea how precious life is, or how fleeting. While most acknowledged they believed they were "better" people for having experienced their loss, they also expressed sorrow for the old self they had left behind. As one participant said, "I would gladly be that silly, naive little girl again if it meant having a living child." The maturity these parents had achieved was bittersweet, neither chosen nor necessarily desired.

Parents' ideas on life, procreation, abortion, and childlessness had undergone subtle shifts. Even if they had not become prolife advocates, they had developed a richer conceptualization of the issues. Parents said, "I used to think it was just a woman's God-given right, but now I see it as a tragedy, even for the woman, because she has lost a relationship, too." Some parents also now understand why adoptees seek birth mothers so fervently; they understand this yearning because of their own experiences of connection and loss.

Several women spoke of changing their mission in life. One woman became a minister, another became a leading member of Caring Beyond, and another returned to school. One woman believed her practice as a physician was much more empathetic and that her patients benefitted from her insights into the connection between mental and physical healing. All spoke of feeling compelled to make their experience worthwhile, to strive to create some good from the ashes of their loss. This need to find a new mission in life seemed to be less urgent for men; although they spoke of being wiser and more complete as humans, none of the men in the study had changed life goals in this way. All respondents spoke of their participation in this study as being motivated by a desire to help, to achieve some higher purpose through sharing their knowledge and pain.

Participants' relationships had also undergone significant changes. Most women with surviving children felt that despite their struggles against overprotection they had become better mothers through their experiences. They claimed to value their living children more because of their loss.

Partnerships were also changed. Although all the women in this study said that there had been difficult times following their losses, they also claimed that their relationships were strengthened because of having negotiated those hard times. Men described themselves as having become better partners, of learning to be more fully human by permitting themselves to be weak as well as strong. It would seem the rite of passage was not only for parents as individuals, but as members of relationships as well.

The emotional journey parents undertake as a result of losing a baby is profound and permanent. These people are heroic, however, in their search for meaning. Despite the overwhelmingly negative nature of their experiences, almost all sought to make something positive out of their loss: some expressed this new direction by investing more in relationships with children and partners; others did so through changed career directions; still others developed a deeper understanding of life and its quirks, enabling them to better serve humanity. These are women and men of true courage, who despite their sense of isolation, fear, injustice, loneliness, anger and sorrow still find it within themselves to get up each morning, renew the task of surviving, and ultimately perform that act with something akin to acceptance in their hearts.

The journey from suffering the initial impact of the loss of one's hoped-for child to finding a meaning in that child's death is a long and complex one.

Chapter 3
What Can Go Wrong (Often) Does: Psychological Factors and Perinatal Death

Rando's (1992, 1993) concept of complicated mourning to organize my analysis. Rando has developed a complex typology of factors that influence the resolution of grief arising from any cause (Rando, 1984). Rando's factors are subsumed within three broad categories: psychological, social, and physiological. First, psychological factors affect how one perceives the loss and hence how one will respond to it. Psychological factors include the nature and meaning of the loss, characteristics of the mourner him/herself, and characteristics of the death. Social factors are the second category of influences that can assist or inhibit the mourning process. Some examples of social factors are the education, occupation and socioeconomic status of the mourners as well as the support systems available to bereaved individuals. Finally, physiological factors contribute to the mourner's ability to work through a loss and include such things as the age of the mourner, his/her physical health, and the influence of drugs. Each of the factors in Rando's typology work either to facilitate or complicate the mourning that bereaved persons need to accomplish (Rando, 1993, pp. 30–31).

In perinatal loss, I believe that the possibility, indeed the probability, exists for "complicated mourning." In addition, I believe there are some areas of perinatal loss that can become complicated in ways that Rando's typology does not fully accommodate, particularly in her discussion of social and physiological factors, which are discussed in Chapters 4 and 5, respectively.

PSYCHOLOGICAL FACTORS

There are a number of psychological factors that contribute to the particular nature of any loss: for example, characteristics pertaining to the meaning of the loss, characteristics of the mourner, and characteristics of the death experience itself. Although Rando identifies these as psychological factors, they are not, in fact, developed solely within and by the individual. All of these factors are affected by the individual's social milieu. For example, parents' religious values, the meanings they attribute to the loss, their sex-role conditioning, the stresses they may be under in addition to the primary loss, indeed all of the factors in Rando's typology, are subject to the influence of societal norms and structures.

Characteristics pertaining to the nature and meaning of the specific loss

The unique nature and meaning of the loss

Rando (1984) states that there is an idiosyncratic meaning to particular losses for each mourner. This meaning can make the loss more painful in ways that might not seem obvious to outsiders. Rando (1984, p. 43) points out that caregivers need to be aware of the significance of the deceased in order to understand the meaning of the loss for mourners. She discusses how some mourners may feel more grief for the deceased than their relationship to the deceased might lead others to expect. The relationship between a parent and a child lost prematurely is not understood by the outside world. I discuss this discrepancy between the nature of a parent's loss and the outside world's understanding of that loss in Chapter 5. In this chapter, I concentrate on exploring the psychological meaning of the loss.

The meanings parents attribute to a perinatal loss have little to do with the personality of or actual relationship with the deceased because that baby is not really "known" before it dies; rather, the meanings that are attached to the loss relate to the symbolic roles and relationships that might have been. The relationship between a parent and child-to-be is highly charged and has a great deal to do with parents' sense of self. Besides their lost babies, parents (particularly mothers) are faced with lost roles. The women I interviewed and who had "just always wanted to have babies" spoke of their careers (and often their marriages) as secondary to their primary goals of childbearing and rearing. For them, facing the prospect of life without mothering meant that they would have to "make do" with a job or childless marriage.

Parents' emotional investments in having a child may go back to their own childhood. For some, the meaning of having a child is tied up with the meaning of their own lives. As one woman said,

> I just knew I would always have a family. It's not just motherhood but that a woman is a certain way. I really did feel that part of being a woman was being a mother, but it was also part of being who I was, and that wasn't just the woman part, it was I wanted to have children.

For this woman, as for other parents, being a parent is tied firmly to their sense of identity. The meaning of the child is far larger than the position that a child actually has in their lives; it cuts to the core of who parents always believed they could, and would, become. The child's death represents the loss of another potential, the potential of the self as parent.

However, I was surprised to discover that many women who grieved deeply were women who did not hold motherhood as a primary goal. For these women, the loss of that part of themselves they valued—the competent, capable woman—led them to question their worth as people and the accuracy of their beliefs about themselves. One professional woman describes this loss of self-confidence poignantly:

> It was a blow. I felt—I really felt that I was not competent, you know, it totally decreased my self-esteem. I had no competence. I couldn't do anything. I couldn't shop for clothes without asking my husband to come with and have a look, and you know "Did this dress look nice?" I couldn't even go grocery shopping without him for the first little while as I just felt that I couldn't even make those kinds of decisions. I felt totally humiliated.

In addition to her loss of a child, this woman suffered the secondary loss of her ability to function and to be competent and decisive in the world. In a sense, she lost her self.

Qualities of the relationship lost

Rando (1984, p. 44) cites attachment as an influence in the mourner's ability to complete grief work, saying that if there is little attachment or dependency in a relationship it will be easier to cope with grief. The attachments that are affected in perinatal grief are less related to what Rando describes as "object-loss" which entails the loss of particular person) than to Rando's "role-loss" which involves a loss of status or function).

Unlike the relationship to someone who has lived, the relationship of a parent to his/her unborn child is not based on instrumental reciprocity. The parent is not "getting" anything in the sense of support or companionship or affection from the unborn baby. Yet, parents' emotional investment in the baby may be enormous. The meaning of their relationship with the baby is not based on "object-loss"; rather, it is invested in hopes and dreams for future actualization. A parent-to-be's loss is a loss of potential, and it means that parents mourn not only for what was, but for what could have been and never will be. They never will know the baby's first smile, the first time he or she says "mama" or "dada," the first halting steps.

Expectations are part of any relationship, but for parents of unborn children, there is little besides expectations on which to base one's feelings. Parents may hold out hopes that their children will have better, happier lives than they did or that they will live out dreams that parents themselves have been unable to fulfill. Parents may also be heavily invested in the ideal of being good parents, perhaps in parenting their children in ways that they were never parented. To lose this opportunity can mean losing the opportunity for their own renewal and healing. One woman explained some of the dreams and hopes she had for her child's future in this way:

> When I found out she was a girl, I was just so happy. I'd always wanted a girl to raise up strong and different from how I was raised. I hoped that I'd be able to provide her with a real sense of her own worth and give her the freedom to be whatever she wanted to be.

The connection to the past through the future was clear when participants spoke about adoption issues. The three adopted women in this sample talked about how having a child was an opportunity for them to be the kinds of parents that their biological parents had not been able to be for them, explaining that their children were the first flesh and blood they had ever known. Losing the chance to parent those children was a loss of connection to both their biological pasts and futures. Conversely, a woman who had formerly given a child up for adoption spoke of hoping to "make amends" for having given up her daughter years earlier by being a "good" parent this time around.

Although there may not be an actual relationship between two individuals (parent and child) in perinatal loss, parents feel a certainty about what that relationship could and should have been. Many parents in my study discussed how they wanted and expected to be good parents. In their concept of themselves as potential good parents, there is a flip side. These parents frequently describe how difficult it is for them to hear about neglectful or abusive parents who have been blessed with living children:

> When I hear about a child being abused or neglected, I get angry that there's no control over how incredibly abusive parents can have dozens of children, and people who would be wonderful parents can't seem to make it through. I wish I was the one who could decide. I would have made a good mother, and I know my husband would have been a good father.

For this mother, as for others, the cruelty of having a child snatched away prematurely is twofold: first, they have been unable to "make it" as parents, despite their expectations of doing a good job; and second, this gift often seems to come undeserved to those who honor it least.

The role the deceased occupied in the mourner's family or social system

Rando's (1984) discussion is tied to the death of a person who has lived, and so her insight in this area reflects the roles that may be left unfilled when an individual dies. The social or family constellation is left out of balance when an individual dies, leaving others to carry on or to find new sources for those functions left unfilled. In the case of a child who has not yet filled those roles, again, there are different implications for the mourner.

Several parents mentioned the hopes they had pinned on their unborn children with regard to their extended families. The value of a male heir to the family name apparently continues to carry weight, even in modern Western families. One woman spoke about how, although there were other grandchildren, her child would have been the first grandson for her husband's parents. She had never felt liked or accepted by her husband's family, and the loss of this male heir represented a loss of her chance to gain favor with the family. Even though she had gone on to bear a subsequent son, the chance for the first grandson had been lost to a sister-in-law, and so her opportunity to cement her position was lost. Two other couples mentioned specifically how painful it had been not to be able to provide male grandchildren, and one woman mentioned how badly her husband had wanted a son.

One woman spoke of her child as a last-ditch effort to save a relationship. For her, the chance to mother her baby was lost along with the chance to continue her marriage. Yet another woman spoke poignantly about being the family black sheep and her hopes that by being a good wife and mother she could finally prove her worth to her family. For these parents, the hoped-for child represented a chance to set right a wrong or to gain some esteem within their families; the deaths of their babies meant the death of their hopes.

Characteristics of the deceased

Again, because Rando (1984) discusses the death of a person who has lived, there are certain implications for those who experience perinatal loss that go beyond her typology. The actual baby has no known characteristics; however, babies are by definition innocent. They have never knowingly harmed anyone, never wittingly been selfish or cruel, never done a bad deed. Thus, a baby's death is extremely difficult to accept, and it can seem particularly unjust to parents. As one woman says,

> I spent a lot of time trying to figure that one out—why my baby had to die. It just never made sense to me that an innocent little baby should get taken.

The death of this woman's baby is that much more poignant because of its senselessness.

Amount of unfinished business between the mourner and the deceased

Rando (1984) describes unfinished business as "those issues that were never addressed or lacked successful closure in the relationship" (p. 50). For example, in the case of an estranged relationship to the deceased, the mourner might have unfinished business in the form of hopes for reconciliation. When possibilities for reconciliation and for setting relationships on the right course are lost, this creates an additional burden in the mourning process.

For parents of a dead baby, unfinished business goes beyond not making amends or resolving differences with the deceased. In choosing to have a child, parents take on a number of promises and responsibilities: to take care of their children, to avoid the same mistakes their parents made, and to love their children unconditionally (Rando, 1993, pp. 613–614). All of these promises are broken, albeit unwillingly, when a baby dies. Parents' inability to follow through on their promises and responsibilities leaves them with a tremendous sense of guilt.

Obviously, there is nothing but unfinished business between a parent and a newborn. Conversely, there is no "finished" business: that is, there are no positive memories of caring for the dead child to counterbalance parents' sense that they have not fulfilled their their responsibilities.

Mourner's perception of the deceased's fulfillment in life

As Rando (1984) states, "The more the mourner perceives the deceased as having had a fulfilling life, the more readily can the death be accepted and the grief work be done" (p. 50). The grief work parents need to accomplish to let their children go is tremendously inhibited by a perception of their child's unfulfilled life.

Parents cannot draw on the comfort of happy memories; they cannot find purpose in the death of an innocent; they cannot point to fulfillment in their children's lives; they often cannot even convince themselves that, if nothing else, their child's life touched and inspired others because of the nonsocial nature of so many perinatal deaths. One mother's comments sum up her feelings about fulfillment:

> When you first become pregnant, you have that hope and those dreams for that child. It doesn't matter that you have 9 months to wait for it—you still start dreaming. What that child's gonna do, where it's gonna go, who it's gonna meet. And it's just like you're left with this, this shattered dream in pieces in front of you. As far as I'm concerned, shattered dreams are the worst part of this entire process.

As she describes the life cycle of her child, we see there is a joyous and hopeful beginning, and there is a grim and stunning end, but there is no middle to this tiny life that can act to counter the shattered dream. There is no passing of milestones, no unfolding of the promise; there is simply nothing.

Number, type and quality of secondary losses

Secondary losses are those losses that occur concurrently or as a result of the primary loss of the loved one. Each of these secondary losses will engender its own grief and mourning, necessitating additional healing (Rando, 1993, pp. 20–21). There were many secondary losses for parents in my study.

Parents who experienced difficulties in the workplace as a result of their losses often suffered the additional loss of their careers. One woman, a career officer in the Army, found her life's work became intolerable after her experiences of pregnancy and loss. Before her loss, her pregnancy was not accommodated in the workplace at all. She was forced to go to field exercises, carry her own 60-pound pack, and live in physically intolerable conditions. When she later began to lose her baby, she felt little control and was unable to fight successfully to get what she needed most to take care of herself and the baby. She believes the Army's treatment of her was a direct cause of the baby's death. Once she returned to work after the death, she discovered that she had been marked within the military system as a trouble-maker and slacker, and the ensuing work climate resulted in her resignation from military service. In effect, she lost not only her baby, but her work, her income and lifestyle, and her future as a career officer.

The nature of secondary losses can be central to the mourner's self-image. As discussed above in the section on the meaning of the loss, it seems that parents whose sole goal was to have children and parents who undervalued parenting versus their career orientation were equally likely to feel the blow of not accomplishing the supposedly "simple" and "natural" act of childbearing. Parents whose identity is tied to beliefs in their competence, good health, and ability to nurture can find that the loss of these beliefs about themselves can be damaging to their self-esteem. This blow to one's self-esteem is a loss to be mourned in and of itself.

Other secondary losses can arise because of the specific hopes and dreams parents pin on their future children. Parents who wish to cement relationships through their children suffer the loss of those possibilities, too. One man, who had hoped to gain some acceptance from his own father by having a son, described how his son's death left him feeling rejected and that he was not good enough. Only after therapy was he able to sort out his feelings and understand that this loss, too, required its own mourning. A woman whose marriage ended spoke of some of the secondary losses attached to her baby's death:

> I was raised in an environment where you lived with your parents until you got married, and you lived with your husband for the rest of your life. So the baby dying was one of the things...it was basically the straw that broke *the* camel's back. That's when all the shit happened.

In addition to mourning her baby, she had the secondary loss of her marriage to mourn as well as the ideal of herself as a good woman who "went from her parents' house to her husband's house" and stayed there through thick and thin.

Sometimes the secondary losses parents had to resolve were not actual; rather, they represented lost illusions. A number of parents described significant shifts in how they understood their childhoods and their families. One woman explains:

> One of the good things that came out of my baby's death was I started going for grief counselling, and it turned into counselling on how to deal with the problems with my mother. It's made me realize this is

the only life I've got, and if I continue to let my parents treat me the way they do, do I want that?

This woman's mother framed the loss as her own, calling friends and relatives and telling them to send cards to her rather than her daughter because her daughter would only be upset by them. She then proceeded to taunt her daughter with how much more support she had received compared to her. The daughter was able to understand that her mother's care for her throughout life had been woefully self-focused: "Because this was a strong enough issue in my life that it was very clear that I was right and she was wrong."

Another woman discussed how, in a long-distance phone call with her brother, her illusions about her family were shattered,

> I only spoke with him to do the usual thing—act nice for my parents. I'd always steered clear of him because he abused me as a kid. Anyway, he had the gall to ask me how my kids were—and he *knew* they'd died! I got off the phone, and I was just crushed because I'd always thought somewhere deep down inside he cared about me!

This woman entered into a long course of therapy to sort out issues of sexual abuse within her family. As she said, "There aren't many Walton family Christmases at my parents' place any more, but they never were anything but a show anyways."

Another illusion that parents may experience as a secondary loss is that they are safe or that the world is a friendly, carefree place. One woman described her life prior to the loss as being without direction or purpose. She ultimately went back to school because she "had a sense that it was time to set a direction for my life. I realized that life is serious and that I had to take my own life more seriously, too. I had that sense that nobody else is going to look after me." She had to work through the loss of the world as a place where she would be taken care of and where things would simply turn out well as a matter of course. Thus, although the illusions parents lost had often been painful or debilitating, they still required working through and still represented secondary losses.

Often, parents only really discovered what unfinished business they had over the death of their child when secondary losses become unbearable. The woman who explored her incest issues, the adoptees who began their adoption searches, the couples who split up over alcohol abuse, the woman who worked through her in-laws' disapproval of her in therapy all believed that these issues stemmed from or pointed out (or both) unresolved issues surrounding the deaths of their children.

Characteristics of the mourner

Coping behaviors, personality and mental health

The focus on coping styles of bereaved individuals subtly reinforces beliefs that normal, healthy individuals will proceed through bereavement smoothly. Generally, in my sample, the personal characteristics of parents as mourners played a minor role in the process of mourning. The members of the sample were functional people. Most of them described their lives as fairly normal, until they lost their babies. Their problem seemed not to be that they were ill-equipped to deal with bereavement, but that the bereavement they faced would be sufficient to lay any individual low. It is important to note that my sample was voluntary, and those people who volunteered were doing so primarily because they wished to share their stories in order to help others; they perceived themselves as people who had come through something terrible and survived and who were willing to share the knowledge and hope that their survival could offer to others.

Rando (1984) suggests that parents who suffer from instability or personality or mental health problems would face additional complications in their mourning process (pp. 45–46). One woman, whose marriage ended, discussed how her husband's alcoholism and violence became steadily worse following their baby's death. She attributed his deterioration to the stress of losing a child. Otherwise, most of the parents I spoke with had little to say about themselves or their coping abilities as contributors to their grief; rather, these were people who, despite usually being well-balanced and in control of their lives, found themselves lost and shaken.

Level of maturity and intelligence

To work through a loss as profound as perinatal loss, parents require an ability to be reflective and insightful. Unfortunately, for many parents, the experience of losing a baby happens when they are young and inexperienced. Often, this is the first truly "bad" thing that has ever happened to them. One woman described herself prior to her loss:

> Like I said, I was very self-centered. And very opinionated. I thought I'd just breeze through pregnancy—no problem! I was very self-centered and a very spoiled child. So for me it was a real ego blow. It was a very hard lesson for me.

For her, and for others, facing loss was made more difficult by youth and naivete. Parents simply did not expect bad things to happen to them, and they had little experience with working through difficulties of this type.

Assumptive world

Rando (1993) explains that "more inherently assumed and socially assigned responsibilities exist in the parent-child relationship than in any other...parents are burdened by unachievable ideals, yet they internalize [them]" (p. 615). I found that the assumptions inherent in becoming a parent did contribute to parental grief. I also found that parental belief in a safe and predictable world left parents feeling personally liable for their children's deaths.

Parents spoke of how naive they were before their loss. They just assumed that they would be able to have children when, and as often, as they wished. They assumed that their health, character, and attitudes would be enough to carry them through pregnancy. They assumed that medical care in pregnancy could be relied upon and that babies simply do not die in pregnancy and childbirth any more. They assumed that once they accepted their pregnancies that would be that. A number of women spoke about their initial ambivalence at being pregnant and how they had to come to terms with their pregnancy. The subtext is that modern women understand (rightly or wrongly) that *they* are the ones who can choose, who can control their own biology. Such assumptions can place an additional burden of guilt and responsibility on parents. The women in this study spoke consistently about being a failure, about being betrayed by their own bodies. They were also consistently dissatisfied with the answers they received from their physicians. Their assumptions that medicine knows and can fix all were again and again proved wrong. Parents whose assumptions are challenged in this way come to see for the first time how precarious life is and how unpredictable their worlds actually are. Understandably, these assumptions represent secondary losses to be worked through.

Previous life experiences, especially past experiences with loss

Rando (1984) discusses how unresolved losses and negative past experiences with loss can hinder effective grieving and how previous experience with similar losses can facilitate grief because the mourner is not a stranger to the experience (p. 47). I found that parent's previous reproductive losses figured quite negatively in their present coping, even if the experience had not been perceived as a negative one at the time. Women who had prior elective abortions discussed the impact of those former life events on their present loss, saying that they suspected some divine intervention was acting to "even the score" or "make them pay" for their acts. In a way, they shouldered an additional burden of blame and responsibility for the loss. For these women, their present loss caused them to reframe the previous decision. One woman explains:

> I don't regret having had that abortion—it was probably the right decision at the time—but I can't help but wonder whether I really understood what I was doing, what an opportunity I was throwing away.

The loss of her desired baby several years later forced this woman to reinterpret her earlier decision in a new light.

Similarly, a woman who had given a child up for adoption spoke about how this new loss was compounded by the older one, saying, "It just seemed that I'd already been hurt enough by having to give up the first one—having this one taken from me too just about killed me." Mourning a child who is put up for adoption is a process that simply does not end (McColm, 1993): that child is perhaps socially dead to you, but he/she is physically alive and lives on in fantasy; so closure in mourning an adoptive child is very difficult to achieve. What this woman knew about grief from dealing with her adopted-out child provided a negative model for her in coming to terms with the new loss. She had already learned that the pain simply never ends.

Expectations about grief and mourning

These parents typically had little prior experience with grief and mourning to assure them that, someday, somehow, the wound will heal enough so that they can carry on and perhaps even experience joy in living once more. For many of the parents in my sample, the funerals of their own children were the first funerals they ever recalled attending. For others, the decision not to go through with a funeral came as a result of a general societal repugnance surrounding the notion of acknowledging death. Many parents failed to understand that having some sort of ritual to commemorate the loss of their children would ultimately prove beneficial. One woman, explaining why she did not have a member of her clergy perform a baptism, said,

> I think I was too scared because I didn't want him to ask us about burial. We didn't want any questions asked; it was traumatic enough, and we didn't want a funeral.

This woman's choice not to observe her child's loss through any ritual was based on an understanding that to do so would only make things *more* traumatic. She believed that if she did not acknowledge the loss formally the pain would somehow be lessened. Unfortunately, parents do come to regret those early decisions, often wishing they had done more, not less, to commemorate the deaths of their children.

In addition to psychological or developmental factors in parental experiences of grief, it is also important to note that the relative youth of parents also gives rise to economic concerns that might not exist for older, more established mourners. Of those parents who had given their children a funeral or cremation, only one had managed to bury their child with a headstone in an appropriate place. For other parents, their children were still not "put to rest." This lack of closure caused ambivalence at best and guilt at worst:

> We couldn't afford at that time to buy a headstone, and funeral homes are such a scam! You get this plot, and then you get all these rules around what you can and can't do, and the cheapest headstone is a thousand bucks. And so we thought, "well, sooner or later, we will," but you know, who has a spare grand? So we never did.

For these parents, their relative youth and financial unpreparedness hampered their ability to "properly" observe rituals of grief and mourning.

The personal unpreparedness of young parents to properly observe rituals of death acts in conjunction with societal norms that fail to acknowledge perinatal loss. For example, none of these parents received financial assistance from their parents to defray funeral costs. Life insurance premiums also did not provide any financial assistance, either privately or through employee benefit plans, again reflecting a societal understanding that the death of these babies was not an important event. This larger social ambivalence was exemplified by one woman's experience of choosing a coffin for her twins. The only coffin she could really afford was made of styrofoam—literally, a disposable container. In her case, the funeral director was understanding and broached the subject of long-term payments for her, so she opted to have both her babies buried together in one, more appropriate coffin. Still, she regretted not being able to bury the girls separately.

Social, cultural, ethnic, generational, and religious/philosophical background

Rando's (1984) elaboration of these influences goes only to the point of advising caregivers to be aware that cultural influences can lead to misunderstanding when the norms of the mourner's culture result in displays of grief that caregivers may not understand, as when one of her stiff-upper-lip British clients shed one sole, yet terribly eloquent tear. While these junctures between cultural norms are interesting, the people I spoke with did not describe being troubled by crosscultural norms in the way Rando describes them. Rather, I found that dominant Western ethics had an internal effect on the people I spoke with, particularly as a result of parents buying into dominant ideas about individualism.

Western culture places a high value on stoicism and self-reliance. For parents who suffer perinatal loss, these values can work in negative ways both before and following the baby's death. A number of women reported how they soldiered on, ignoring warning signs, insisting they were okay, despite fatigue and pain and "feeling unwell." One woman described waiting until the very last minute before going to a neighbor to ask for a ride to the nearest hospital, over an hour's drive away. She had been in labor at home for over 24 hours, insisting she was fine, not wishing to be a burden to her husband and family members who could have driven her sooner. Another described taking a taxi to the hospital. When the driver, noticing she was carrying a little overnight bag, asked her if she was going on shift, she simply replied "yes," although her contractions were by this time coming regularly. The minimizing that is a part of women's stoicism often left them with feelings of guilt—that perhaps they should have done more sooner, more insistently to take care of themselves and their pregnancies.

Following the loss, individuals' beliefs in stoicism and individualism can hamper their ability to reach out for support. Although almost everyone in this sample had heard of Caring Beyond, many of them admitted they had not attended any meetings or contacted the group, saying that for them grief was a private matter and that attending a support group seemed weak or inappropriate. Others spoke of wanting to go back to work right away because that way they could just get on with their lives and get things back to normal. Unfortunately, the unwillingness to reach out to others and the desire to shoulder the load as soon as possible often had long-term repercussions for parents. Many talked about going back to work too soon and only really knowing that much later. One man says,

I was a basket case. I really thought I needed to be back at my job, someplace where I knew I could be in control. Of course, once I got there, I started totally screwing up, which just made me feel worse.

Because he failed to acknowledge just how injured he was, he suffered an additional blow to his self-esteem, which compounded his loss.

Religious affiliations can be both helpful and harmful in parental mourning processes. A number of parents had to struggle to have their babies baptized, sometimes unsuccessfully. This led them to question their faith and to feel that their losses were not important, even to their church. For others, seemingly "pat" answers from clergy members about why these things happen left them deeply dissatisfied. It really seemed as though there were two factors at work here: how well-affiliated the individuals are to their church and church community and how insightful the individual clergy member is. Parents who, for the first time in years, approached their churches for answers or who were questioning their faith in any case, often were disappointed by their clergy member's attempts to comfort them and in how little support they received from church members.

The parents I interviewed had often experienced breaks in faith following their losses or had spent at least some time questioning that faith. Often these breaks in faith arose from parents' perceptions of injustice. Not only do parents question the fairness of a God who would deny them the joy of parenting, but the unfairness of their babies' deaths often contrasts with injustices in the church itself. Each time a parent picks up a newspaper and reads of abuse, they are reminded that the innocent are often the most vulnerable, while the powerful remain unassailable. One woman was poignant in discussing this juncture between innocence and injustice:

> If anything my belief in the Catholic church deteriorated further after my baby died. For a number of reasons, for my personal experience...and the stories of priests who have been abusing children in one way or another for years and years and never being held accountable, and the church coming in to protect them. And my father's tithing, going to pay for the lawyers' fees to get these guys off.

This woman feels her world has turned upside down. An innocent baby dies senselessly, other children are abused by those to whose care they are entrusted, spiritual leaders are proved to be moral bankrupts, and good people unwittingly support them in their guilty secrets. For a woman with such a worldview, there is small comfort in believing that "these things happen for a reason."

Sex role conditioning

Rando (1984, p. 48) states male sex-role conditioning complicates mourning because of traditional values that condition men to be controlled and to avoid the expression of feelings. The stories men told and the stories women told about them supported Rando's theory. Men who believe that their best and most appropriate course of behavior is to be stoic, matter-of-fact, and resilient pay a double price. First, they may not be able to process their own mourning, and second, they run the risk of alienating themselves from their partners. Most of the men I interviewed admitted that problems had occurred in their marriages because they "failed to be as sensitive" as they perhaps should have been.

This group of men all described returning to work as soon as possible afterward and defined their primary role during and following the loss as one of supporting and caring for their wives. As one man said, "I was just waiting for her to come back to the person that I knew before. I knew it would take her some time, but I was prepared to wait for it." These men, at least initially, saw the loss as their wife's loss and hence took a long time to understand and respond to their own feelings of sorrow and pain. One woman described how her husband required a second crisis to finally deal with his own grief over their dead son:

> At first my husband did everything to support me. I was really the focus. After that passed, he was very distant—he just seemed to be running away from his own feeling. Then he went on a peacekeeping mission to Yugoslavia, which I think brought his own pain forward—seeing all those children. Since then I think he's pretty well gone through his own healing.

Not all fathers needed a catalyst as dramatic as watching other children suffer in war, but for most men, it seems that a wake-up call was often necessary before they were willing to look at their own feelings. Many women described pivotal events or discussions when they "called" their husbands on their apparent lack of emotion and the subsequent healing process that "call" engendered. Sometimes, these catalysts occurred months or even years after the actual deaths. Sometimes, the wake-up call was the threatened end of their marriage.

Rando's (1984, p. 48) discussion of complications that arise from female sex-role conditioning focuses on the difficulties some women may have in expressing their anger. I did not find that the women in my study were particularly "stuck" in not feeling or expressing anger, but I did find other examples of sex-role conditioning that hindered women's ability to mourn.

Pronatalism figured prominently in complicating women's mourning. Women who subscribe to dominant cultural themes of bearing children as a status passage to adulthood or who believe that the most "sacred" or morally good thing that a woman can do is have babies find they need to discover what it now means, to them, to be a woman. More subtle is the pressure that pronatalist values can exert on women who are ambivalent about motherhood or who did not want the pregnancy. One woman, who did not want to be pregnant, tells the following story:

> I wanted to discuss abortion because I was tired of it and I wanted to end the pregnancy. And I don't know if I would have done it or not, but I wanted to discuss it with [my husband], and he just would not hear of it. And I was angry with him for a long time for not allowing me to even explore whether that might be an option. And he felt so guilty for being mad at me, so there were all those feelings in there that carried forward.

This woman's ambivalence about being pregnant came into conflict with her husband's traditional Catholic values about abortion, at the cost of communicating her feelings and sharing decisions with her partner. As a mother, the range of feelings she was permitted to feel did not include a wish to end the pregnancy. This conflict remained a sore spot between the couple, and it was only resolved when some of the husband's family-of-origin issues led him into therapy.

Age

The age of mothers, in particular, can have an impact on perinatal grief. For some of the mothers in my sample, this loss was viewed as their last opportunity to have a child. For parents who have made plans for specific family sizes or who have made career decisions to accommodate anticipated children, there are secondary losses. Several women discussed how not having any more children had forced them to rethink their own careers much earlier than they might have desired.

Advanced maternal age at the time of loss meant that for some there never would be a child, and for others, they would be raising an "only" child. One woman described the stigma she feels in raising a single child:

Nobody ever asks me if I have one child, it's always "do you have *just* the one?" as though somehow I'm shirking. It's really painful for me to have to explain that our family size is not our choice, but because we couldn't have any more.

This woman, with "only" one child in the family, feels pressure to have more children. Parents with no children feel pressure as well. One woman, childless, described how she dealt with family and social pressure to have a family: "That stopped real fast. I called a meeting and just told them I wasn't going to have any kids! I think I was so strong, nobody dares to ask anymore."

For several parents in this study, fertility issues compounded their mourning process. Knowing that one may never be able to have another child because of difficulties conceiving or because of ongoing medical problems or because of maternal age can mean that parents may see this loss as the end of the road in terms of parenting possibilities. Such a juncture can mean that parents become aware, possibly for the first time in their lives, of their own mortality. Certainly, it can bring people face to face with their own lack of control over their lives and their bodies.

Developmental stage of life, lifestyle, and sense of meaning and fulfillment

Parents can hope that having a child will somehow "complete" them, particularly if they have deferred personal goals in order to have a family. Parents who have given up careers or who have only ever wanted the career of childrearing can experience the loss of their infant as the loss of their life's meaning. For some parents, getting on with a career or going back to school are simply not attractive alternatives.

If the dead baby was the last or only possibility a woman has for becoming a mother, that death can mean the end of hope. One woman describes how this situation affected her:

I guess in a lot of ways our picture of what the ideal family would be— we had spaced everything, it was just so much the way we wanted it. And then when we lost the first baby, that was all my husband commented on—that it would have been so perfectly timed. And then we lost another. And when that baby died, it was like we had that one last chance where we could have it that it wouldn't space so far apart. But now we're at a point, like my husband doesn't want to have a fourth anyways, because it's been so long since we've had a baby around, and [my youngest son] is 5, and I'm in school. Like, it's just too late.

This woman and her husband feel the moment is past for having another child. Too much time, too much sorrow, and too much accommodation to the loss make undertaking another pregnancy undesirable. Women like this one, who are too old to take on another pregnancy or who feel the "right" time is lost, have an additional burden of regret: their chances are gone.

Parental lifestyles can affect what resources are available to the mourning process. Couples who are not stable undoubtedly experience additional burdens in resolving their grief. Two couples in this study had been experiencing problems with alcoholism prior to the loss: one couple's marriage ended within 2 years of the death, and the other couple separated for almost a year, reconciling only after the husband had gone through treatment.

The parents in this study who moved around a great deal had few resources to call upon when they needed social support, finding themselves isolated and far from family and friends. Parents whose lifestyle is not socially accepted experienced a different kind of isolation. The lesbian couple in my study, for example, kept their loss secret from family members because they "did not want to make anybody happy" as a result of it. The censure they experienced in even trying to have children led them to fear that people would formulate their loss not just as "one of those things," but would actually see it as a moral victory because they viewed the pregnancy as immoral.

Presence of concurrent stresses or crises

Rando (1984, p. 54) simply says that ongoing stresses unrelated to the death may add to the bereavement experience. In this sample, a number of stressors typical to people in their childbearing and childrearing years contributed to complicated perinatal mourning. Parents with other children at home had problems finding care for their children while mothers were hospitalized and finding care for those children prior to their losses in order to rest and accommodate troubled pregnancies. Once the babies died, parents of small children were also faced with the task of explaining difficult situations to young siblings. Parents felt they had let these children down, that they had shattered their innocence, and that they were responsible for the loss felt by their living children.

Additionally, caring for children following the loss was often beyond the coping skills of parents; parents often described feeling they neglected their children while struggling to deal with their grief, creating an additional burden of guilt. For women who have very small children and who stay at home, isolation can be an additional problem. The women in my sample who stayed at home with their children had little opportunity to interact with other adults who may have provided sympathy or, at the very least, opportunities for diversion.

Characteristics of the death

The death surround

Rando (1984) defines the death surround as the "location, type of death, reason for the death and degree of preparation for it" (p. 50) and says that the more acceptable the surround (i.e., the deceased is older, dies after an anticipatory period, and dies in familiar and comforting surroundings), the more easily grief work will be accomplished. Children who die at or near birth typically possess none of the qualities that ease the grief mourners experience. I have discussed the age and lack of fulfillment of the deceased above and will discuss the aspect of preparation for death in discussing anticipatory grief. Therefore, I will limit my analysis in this section to the actual physical death surround and how hospitalization and this medicalization of the deaths acted to compound parental pain.

With the exception of one woman whose losses were in the first trimester, all of the parents in this sample suffered their losses in a medical setting. Besides experiencing the actual loss in a hospital, confirmations of the death or intimations that death was imminent were often experienced in hospital or clinical settings. Thus, medical institutions were the surround for experiences before, during and following the deaths. At each of these junctures, there were recurring problems that ultimately contributed to complications in perinatal mourning.

The ultrasound clinic was consistently problematic for women who suspected problems with their pregnancies. I frequently heard stories about insensitive ultrasound technicians and radiologists. It seems that ultrasound technicians are not permitted to disclose the results of ultrasounds to patients; rather, the radiologist will be called in to give parents bad news. Parents, however, *know* when something is wrong with their ultrasound, even while the technician is denying it or trying to minimize the situation. Once the radiologist is brought in to confirm the parents' worst fears, things do not generally go much better:

> So the doctor came in and said, "Things aren't looking good." And he just kept shaking his head and said, "Well, you know, we'll have to have your family doctor call you." And I said, "Well, I want to know, what do you mean by 'not good?'" And that's when he said, "Well, the baby isn't living—your family doctor will call you." And that was that.

Once the news had been delivered, she was left alone. She sat stunned for a while until someone finally came and said, "What are you waiting for?" so she stirred herself, got herself dressed, and drove herself home. For this woman, the impact of what she felt was acted out in an environment that not only did not support her understanding of the loss, but literally ignored it as an event of any importance.

A very common experience was that once problems began to present themselves parents became involved with physicians who were not known to them. In this sample, only three couples had their own physician attend them in any capacity during the birth and death of their children. Perhaps this is because the timing of these events is unexpected. Nonetheless, having to deal with physicians and obstetricians who knew next to nothing about the parents' physical, social or psychological backgrounds was often an additional burden.

Obstetricians particularly came in for a great deal of criticism. It seems that obstetricians are often called in on cases that are not progressing normally, and their demeanor was often perceived by parents as abrasive and self-important. A number of women recalled refusing to cooperate with particular obstetricians, feeling that they were being bossed around or were being treated as a mere body rather than a person facing an extremely difficult situation. Going through labor and being uncertain of the outcome or knowing that the worst has already occurred can be greatly facilitated when parents trust the practitioner in charge. Having to deal with a difficult and powerful stranger without that bond of trust created significant stress for parents.

Hospital efforts to provide a supportive and understanding environment for parents facing perinatal loss have met with considerable success. Nonetheless, for some parents, there were problems at the hospital that compounded rather than mitigated the pain of the loss. Lay literature on miscarriage and stillbirth is clear that parents should be encouraged to hold and say goodbye to their babies. This encouragement is not always offered:

> When I delivered, the nurse quickly wrapped it up in a green sheet and said quickly, "Let's just take this away now." And I said, "I need to see it, so can you please just not—just leave it here." But I remember her sort of standing on my left, and she held this green sheet with the baby, and after a couple of minutes she said, "Okay, well that's enough for now." And she covered him up, and off she went.

This woman's greatest regret was that she had not properly said goodbye to her son, yet she received no real guidance from the nurse who attended her.

In fact, her natural desire to hold her child was actively discouraged. She never did learn what became of her son's body—he was simply whisked away and disposed of.

After the death of her son, this woman was left on the Labor and Delivery ward:

> They left me there for probably a good 4 hours, and I lay there and listened to all the other women screaming through their pushing and then screaming with elation. I heard all these babies crying. And I've never felt so put down and so humiliated and so alone in all my life.

This series of events occurred within the last 4 years at a hospital that has a good reputation for perinatal loss support. Long after her loss, with the help of the staff social worker she began seeing, an informal investigation was made into why things went so terribly wrong for her at the hospital. The explanation was that the death occurred on a weekend when the ward was short-staffed: a temporary glitch in the system. Yet for this mother, the opportunity to properly say goodbye was lost forever.

Timeliness

Rando (1984, p. 51) describes a timely death in terms of whether death occurs at the end of a long and fruitful life and if death was expected to occur. Obviously, neither of these things are present in the death of an infant; there is no fulfillment, and the death often comes as a shock. Thus, grieving for these infants becomes more difficult because of the "wasted potential" of their tiny lives and the unpreparedness of the mourner.

There is another aspect regarding the timeliness of a baby's death that is pertinent to perinatal loss. In the section on the meaning and nature of perinatal loss, I discussed some of the intangible promises that a baby might hold for parents: for example, they may wish to live out unfulfilled fantasies or desires through their children. There are also tangible fantasies that parents have for their babies: for example, baby's first Christmas, baby's first birthday, baby's first day at Kindergarten. When parents come face to face with reminders of these hoped-for milestones, they can suffer from what Rando (1993, p. 64) calls Sudden Temporary Upsurges of Grief (STUGS). Even parents who have done all the "right" things in holding, saying goodbye to, and commemorating their lost babies are subject to STUGS. Particularly because parents of dead babies are of an age when most of their friends and family members are in "baby-mode," they are frequently confronted with cues that elicit renewed pain. If the desired baby was going to be born at the same time as a best friend's baby or was to be born at the same time as a new cousin, seeing those children and watching them grow up over the years can provide a constant, living narrative of what was lost for parents of babies who die. For mothers who planned to have a baby along with another close woman friend, the death of their child often meant the death of a friendship as well.

Psychosocial context within which the death occurs

We cannot choose the timing of death, but often, we hope to choose the timing of life. Many of the parents in this study discussed how their babies were to have been born at a certain time for a variety of reasons: because the best friend was pregnant, because the age gap between siblings would have been "perfect," because of a desire to compress (or protract) women's stay-at-home years, and/or because it was hoped that an ailing grandparent would live long enough to see the grandchild born. With the death of the baby, these hopes died, too.

Amount of mourner's anticipation before the death, degree of suddenness and length of illness prior to the death

Rando (1993) tells us that a mourner who expects the death and has time to prepare for it is able to maintain a sense of their world as a predictable place. Without this, mourners can be left feeling that a blow can occur without warning at any time (Rando, 1993, p. 52). With the exception of one couple whose child died following a 2-week-long illness and three women whose premature deliveries were preceded by lengthy hospitalizations for pregnancy complications, parents in this study had hardly any time to prepare for the loss. The experience of the death was often described as unfolding "at breakneck speed." Parents recounted that "things were happening so fast that we had no time really to sit down and talk about what we really wanted to do— it was just too late for any of that." In fact, the urgency of the births was often a direct result of medical intervention. None of the women in my study actually lost their babies during delivery; parents were either aware that the baby was dead before labor even began, or in the case of prematurely ruptured amniotic sacs, the baby was too young to survive labor. In either case, almost all of the women in this sample received Pitocin® to speed up the labor process. Perhaps this is because physicians (and, in fairness, parents, too) believe that getting the birth over with as quickly as possible is the most desirable option. There is also a fear that infection can occur as the baby begins to deteriorate in utero or as bacteria enter through the torn amniotic sac. Nonetheless, the speed of most parents' experience of discovering the death, deciding to induce, and living through a chemically-accelerated birth left them with little time for preparation or discussing what is happening to them. Again, parents were left with regrets that might have been avoided if they had just a few hours longer and a lot more guidance from people who could help them through the myriad of decisions they face.

Mourner's perception of preventability

In her analysis, Rando (1984) claims that ambiguity about whether the death could have been prevented or whether the griever could have changed things increases grief and guilt. I found this connection borne out repeatedly, particularly by the women in this study who continue to go over what they could have done or should have done to prevent the baby's death. This particular burden was often added to by interactions with medical personnel.

Women often suspected they were having problems with their pregnancies because of decreased fetal movement or through leakage of amniotic fluid. A number of women described how their concerns and complaints prior to the deaths of their children were ignored by medical personnel. One woman went to her doctor complaining of decreased fetal movement and was given a pat on the wrist and told to go home. She woke up the next morning to no fetal movement and gave birth later that day to a full-term stillborn daughter. The grief she feels over her daughter is compounded by rage at the doctor who simply would not listen to or investigate her complaints. One of the hardest things for her to resolve has been the feeling of impotence and rage she has over not being heard.

Women struggled to be taken seriously in hospitals as well. A woman who had a Shirodker suture (a thick cord that is run through the cervical opening like a drawstring when the weight of the baby in utero causes the cervix to open prematurely) in place described how she was unable to convince anyone in the hospital to take her warnings about the suture seriously:

> I kept saying to them, "Look, if this baby's gonna come—and it will soon, because that's how labor is for me—you'd better get this suture out!" And everybody kept smiling and assuring me that it would get taken care of. Meanwhile, they did absolutely nothing.

This woman went into speedy labor, as she predicted, and indeed the suture remained in place. Ultimately, because the baby was being pushed against a sealed cervical opening, he died of cerebral hemorrhage. At 26 weeks, the baby may have survived, but because of brain damage incurred during the birth, the parents were advised to let him die. Further, the trauma of the birth caused excessive blood loss and postpartum infection for the mother, requiring her to stay in hospital for several weeks following the birth. She is convinced she is too damaged to conceive another child and says, "Even if I could, I would never want to put myself or my partner through that again."

There is a sense of screaming into the void for parents who try to redress medical omissions and commissions. Most parents do not even feel it is worthwhile to approach medical personnel in hopes of getting any satisfaction. The woman who was ignored by her physician when she presented complaints of decreased fetal movement did make an attempt to push for an apology. She got no further than the office receptionist, who told her,

"Well, Dr. W. feels very bad about it," and I got really angry at the receptionist and said, "It is different. She does *not* feel badly. She doesn't even *know* what it feels to feel badly—let her try and feel what I feel. And the receptionist said, "Well, L., you can't expect *that*."

What parents do expect in these situations is an acknowledgment that a mistake has been made, that there is some responsibility on the part of medical practitioners, and that this acknowledgement implies a promise that it will not happen again. One woman described her physician as "the incredible Teflon man—each time I bring the topic up, it just slides right off him...he shrugs and says these things just happen." Perhaps because medical personnel are trained to be hierarchical in their doctor-patient relationships, perhaps because of the fear of liability suits that might come as a result of an admission of culpability, or perhaps because the medical establishment is simply not willing to accept its own fallibility, acknowledgements of responsibility and apologies are never offered.

The perceived shirking of responsibility can counteract positive or well-intended efforts by the medical profession. The woman who went into labor with an intact Shirodker suture describes her feelings when she received a follow-up phone call from the maternity ward's Assistant Head Nurse,

I'm sure she meant well, but when she called to see how I was doing, all I could think about was that she had a hell of a lot of nerve to call me up and offer sympathy when, after all, it was her staff that killed my baby.

The discrepancy between parents' experiences and the medical response to it is extremely painful as it leaves parents no place to direct their rage. It can also leave parents feeling guilty and confused when medicine does extend a supportive hand.

Anticipatory grief and involvement with the dying person

Anticipatory grief occurs when mourners are aware before the death that it is imminent and use the remaining time with the dying person to accomplish some mourning of the loss. During this time, mourners may take the opportunity to say good-bye and may try to make amends to the dying person (Rando, 1984, p. 53). One set of parents in my sample had this type of opportunity. Their son became extremely ill right after birth and, after a tense and heroic struggle, succumbed to encephalitis. The course of his illness was registered in small steps: First the baby was sick, then a second and a third and then innumerable health crises ensued over the passing days. By the time they finally decided to take him off life support, there was so much brain damage that to do otherwise seemed cruel. These parents had an extremely difficult process, yet they were able to see in increments that their son would die, were able to let him go bit by bit, and this actually facilitated their grief.

Most parents in this study, however, were not able to prepare for the end gradually. One mother of a stillborn child described the jealousy she felt hearing of another woman's whose baby had died after 4 days, saying,

That woman had 4 days with her child. And I was so intensely jealous. And that made me realize a lot more when people told me they had early miscarriages. I used to think they did not know what it feels like to lose a baby. Now I think they do. More so. I recognize that they may feel envious of the fact that I got to hold my baby, that I got to know what sex it was, that I got have the emotional attachment to my child. The more you get, the better off you are. And it goes the other way in the sense that the more I got, the more I lost.

Her discussion reflects a general consensus among parents in this study that every extra living second you got with your baby was a precious gift, while, ironically, every additional day of pregnancy made losing a baby that much harder.

CONCLUSION

Rando (1984, 1992, 1993) presents an extensive range of psychological factors that affect mourning. In this chapter, I have explored each of Rando's psychological influences to explain how and why parents of dead babies are at risk for complicated mourning. The psychological nature of these factors is not purely an internal matter, but it rests on what parents believe and how they interpret the events they encounter before, during and after their loss. Thus, although the factors above are psychological, they are enacted and interpreted in social and cultural settings. Rando also presents social and physiological factors that contribute to enhancing or complicating mourning. As will be seen, these factors are also not purely social or physical, but their impact depends on how individuals interpret them and what meaning they attach to those influences. Thus, social and physiological factors carry a psychological component as well.

Chapter 4
Silence and Empty Arms:
Social Factors in Perinatal Death

According to theorists in the sociology of emotions, many emotions are not universal; rather, they are particular to time and space (Badinter, 1980; Hochschild, 1983; Thoits, 1987). Grief, too, is affected by social conditions. According to Lofland (1985, pp. 174–175), the level of grief felt is shaped by the level of significance of the one who dies, the situation surrounding the death, and the particular individual experiencing the loss. She goes on to say that the overarching force that shapes grief is the interactional (or social) setting in which these elements unfold. But just as psychological factors are not purely personal, social factors are not purely external to the individual; they are interpreted and altered by the individual in social interaction. Thus, individuals feel and interpret grief through a complex mix of psychological, situational and social forces that act and react upon one another.

According to Hochschild (1983), we all take for granted "that there are rules or norms according to which feelings may be judged appropriate to accompanying events. We are (also) aware what are our rights and obligations around certain events and their attendant feelings" (p. 59). Mourners are expected to feel sad at the funeral and to become less sad as time goes on. They are encouraged to display the appropriate affect, at the appropriate time, and in the appropriate place. When parents expressed their felt emotions, they often encountered "feeling rules" that let them know how inappropriate it was for them to express their emotions. These disjunctures between parents' felt emotions and the socially imposed feeling rules around perinatal loss occurred at all levels of interaction: in parents' marriages, in their families, in their workplaces, and in their religious and secular communities.

In Chapter 3, I discussed how psychological factors can affect the mourning process at every level of Rando's typology. As I noted, psychological factors are not entirely private in nature; rather, they are learned and acted out in response to social settings and norms.

SOCIAL FACTORS

Mourner's social support system and the recognition, validation, acceptance, and assistance provided by its members

Within the family

Rando (1984) explains that social support is "based on how the griever and the deceased are valued by members of the social system" (p. 54, italics added). The gaps in social support that parents experienced occurred primarily because of a discrepancy between their valuation of the deceased and the lack of value others attributed to the loss. In other words, the death of their babies was not a "social death" to others in the parents' support networks.

For almost all the parents in my study, the level of social support they desired and felt they needed was nowhere near the actual support they received. For some parents, this discrepancy arose because of physical barriers: for example, when parents were isolated from friends or immediate family due to geography. For many parents, however, the discrepancy between desired level of support and actual support received occurred either because people made inappropriate attempts at support or because they simply failed to understand that any support was required for parents whose neonate dies.

As I discussed in Chapter 2, the support that women and men were able to provide one another was often severely limited by differences in their personal beliefs about gender roles. There were also structural and role-imposed influences that were detrimental to positive communication and resolution for partners. Men's return to the workplace, for example, was generally mandatory, so even if the men did not hold private values of instrumentalism and "getting on with life," they felt tremendous pressure to act according to these societal values. This swift return to "normal" by husbands often took place at the same time that women were sick or recuperating at home, creating additional distance between partners.

Women consistently talked about how isolated they felt following their losses and how distant they felt from their husbands. Part of this isolation occurred as a function of the different lives couples led following their loss: Men returned to business as usual, while women typically had more time to reflect on their losses because they received sick leave or maternity benefits or because they were stay-at-home parents. Lofland (1985) speculates that intense, modern-day grief "could only occur among persons who have access to considerable periods of solitude and privacy and who have considerable time and space discretion" (p. 180). She contends that the isolation and time alone available to people in our culture permits introspection in a way that was not possible in other times and cultures. This may be one structural reason why women describe themselves as being more intense than their partners in their grieving; they simply have the possibility in terms of time and space to process their grief immediately after the loss. Indeed, a number of women did talk about how their partners' grief *did* get processed eventually, often triggered by some unrelated event, such as being in combat in Yugoslavia or incidents of abuse. Perhaps if fathers, too, were given time from the workaday world to honor their experiences, couples might be more successful in working through their grief together rather than in silent solitude.

The structuring of men's grief reactions goes beyond simply not being granted paternity leave; it occurs informally as well. Men are consistently told to be strong for their wives, locking them into a supportive rather than primary role, and sending a message that this is the wife's loss and men have no grief of their own to resolve. Thus, stoicism is socially reinforced for men, perhaps accounting for some of the silence that causes wives to feel isolated. One woman describes a typical interaction her husband experienced:

> He gets angry a lot more than I do, and I think this is very male....He told a fellow down the street our baby died, and the guy said, "Oh. Bummer." When [my husband] came home, he was just seething. I laughed when he told me, and he was, like "That's not funny!" but I understand that people don't know what to say.

This man is being given two very clear messages. The first message, typical of many such comments parents reported, is from the neighbor who expresses that the death of his baby really is kind of a drag but not something that bears discussion or emotional outpouring. The second message is perhaps less typical because it comes from his wife, but it nonetheless confirms that he really should let these inappropriate comments roll off his back and get used to having his feelings minimized by others.

The messages women receive are different. Women with surviving children consistently report being told not to feel badly because they at least have their other children to compensate for their loss. One woman talks about how these comments made her feel:

> People say "Oh well, you can have another" or "you're lucky, you have two healthy babies already." But I did not feel lucky. And I felt guilty somewhat when people said that because I did not feel—at that point I had not reached a place where I could value my children more. I was too busy grieving the one I'd lost.

These comments not only do nothing to explain away women's pain, but they also imply that women who do persist in feeling sad are somehow undervaluing their living children. A number of women spoke about how they "knew" they should not be feeling so sad, but they just could not seem to help themselves. Being told that one should not feel unhappy because one has a living child or because one is young enough to have more pregnancies or because "at least you have your health and a good marriage" does little more than deny the very real feelings experienced by women. These messages, or feeling rules, also induce guilt in women for even having those grief feelings because, after all, they have so much for which to be thankful.

In addition to inducing guilt over their feelings, social messages directed at women tend to induce guilt for their behavior, particularly while pregnant. There is a stigma to losing a baby that is situated in women's bodies. Women described being told that they had their miscarriages because during the pregnancy they smoked, continued to work, took too much on at home, weighed too much (or too little), or were too nervous to carry the baby to full term. Women are even held accountable for pregnancy complications by their partners. One man described how his wife's third pregnancy became complicated following the stillbirths of two previous children:

> It was again around 19–20 weeks. Whether it was in her head or whatever, there were some pains and tenderness, and she ended up being in the hospital for 16 weeks, under supervision, on her back. Her cervix was softened, and I think they had to divert labor at least once. I think it was all because she was just getting upset about the chain of events.

Despite medical evidence to the contrary, this husband assumed the pregnancy complications stemmed from his wife's emotional state and were, therefore, within her control.

Even when pregnancy loss occurs as a result of physical rather than emotional problems, guilt messages can come from partners. Another husband openly discussed the issue of responsibility when physical problems with the mother accounted for pregnancy loss:

> In our instance, it was not the babies that were the problem, it was the mother who wasn't able to hold the kids. It was—unfortunately—a defect in her. Though you don't ever want to say it was her fault, but really if you have to put any blame on why it happened, unfortunately it falls on her body. So even though you don't want to look at it as blame, blame does come into play, and since the babies were normal, unfortunately as my wife puts it, "There's nothing I could have done to improve or correct it."

Although this man clearly states that he does not blame his wife, he also clearly states that her failings caused the losses. I have to admit that as a woman who has lost perfectly healthy babies for undiscovered reasons I felt extremely uncomfortable hearing this discussion of blame. I can only imagine how his framing the loss as his wife's responsibility might have affected her. In fact, her reported comment, that she could have done nothing to improve or correct things, sounds like a plea for absolution.

When men are given messages to act like men, they are told to keep their feelings in, to shoulder the responsibilities of manhood, and to take their blows on the chin without flinching. When women are given messages to act like women, they are told to be grateful for their surviving children, to look forward to replacing the lost child as soon as possible, or to look within themselves for the causes of the loss. When these messages are internalized, communication and sharing grief become enormously complicated. Men become distant and instrumental, while their wives descend into an abyss of guilt and self-doubt. The net result is a resounding silence between parents at a time when good communication is needed most. Small wonder that many parents report difficulties in their marriages following the loss.

Within the extended family

Attendance at the funeral, sending a card, remembering a child's birthdate or due date, including their name on family trees, being willing to talk about the dead child, all are instances where family members can provide validation and recognition of the loss parents have suffered. Unfortunately, family members were not necessarily helpful when these opportunities arose.

Many women spoke of how even their mothers had not managed to attend the funeral.

The issue of social support seems to rest on expectations and disappointments. Three women whose mothers were unable to be at the funeral or to attend the death said their mothers' absences were due to other, more pressing duties elsewhere. One woman's mother was in South Africa, another's was in California helping out with a sister's new baby, and a third's mother was in England attending to the health needs of her father. These women accepted these reasons for nonattendance as valid, and as a result, they felt their mothers had been supportive. They described these mothers as having been *willing* but *unable* to offer concrete support due to circumstances beyond their control, and that perceived willingness was enough to provide them with comfort. Framing the experience as beyond the supporter's control rather than a deliberate snub lessened the impact of actual nonsupport.

For parents, however, who expected family support yet received little, the disappointment was very painful. Parents commonly described how "every time I brought the subject up, my parents would change the subject." One woman who asked her mother why she had not attended the funeral was told "because it was too painful for me." Another woman describes how, 3 months after her baby died, she finally told her mother she was hurt at the lack of support she had received:

> My mother actually said to me, "Well, if you have such a problem with that, why don't you phone Ann Landers."...My parents never sent a card until 3 months later. Then my father and mother got on the phone to my husband and said they were worried about me because they thought I was so weird about this, that I was going to end up in the loony bin.

Even when this woman was willing to stand up and ask for what she needed, she was met with silence and denial. Instead of being given support for her loss, her expression of how she felt was deemed pathological, with the implication being that by 3 months after the death a sane person would no longer be upset and harping on it. The hidden message is that the appropriate behavior would be silence—if she cannot get over it, at least she could have the decency to keep it to herself.

When grieving parents are either directly or indirectly told that their feelings are not appropriate or that their handling of the situation has been inadequate, particularly by members of their own family, the additional pain can make grief resolution very difficult. Many parents described harboring resentments against family members who did not attend funerals or who failed to send flowers or remember birthdates. One woman described how her parents had never contributed to a church fund that had been set up in her child's memory:

> They did not contribute because they thought that was a gift, not something they were required to do. Well, it's true—it was a gift, but the point is, you *do* that when someone dies. They donated to a friend of my mothers' son's account that died recently, and he was about 35. So, you know, it's different. This was a baby that was never born.

This harkens back to Doka's (1987) discussion of disenfranchised grief and the concept of a social death (Mulkay, 1993). Because the death of this infant was not socially real to the grandparents, the traditional observances were not made, and the parents were hurt again by the nonrecognition of their loss. In the grandparents' understanding, the baby did not really die; hence, the parents should not really grieve. When these gaps in understanding occur within the framework of one's family, where the expectations of support are high, the pain is terrible.

Friends and acquaintances

A number of women spoke about feeling stigmatized as mothers who have given birth to dead babies. Women who have borne still babies are not permitted to share in conversations about their births or pregnancies, nor are they permitted to participate in motherly activities. One woman describes how she felt:

> There were a couple of women who had just had babies around the time that mine was born. And they were absolutely terrified of me! For some strange reason they were scared, like what happened to my daughter was "catching." And that *hurt*!

Perhaps the stigma she felt arose from others' intentions to protect her from additional pain. A common social understanding of grief is that the mourner would be better off not to encounter any reminders of the loss, assuming, in a sense, "out of sight, out of mind." Yet this woman, after her baby died, wanted nothing more than to hold a living baby. At a party several weeks after her loss, she did hold a 2-week-old child, and the mother whisked the baby out of her arms, saying, "I'll hold the baby for you. You don't have to see that baby if you don't want to." Not only did the grieving mother not get the physical comfort she sought, but she received an additional blow, feeling that her desire to touch another child was neither healthy or desirable.

Another woman discussed the experience of having everyone around her ignore or deflect any discussion of her loss:

> [People] believe that if they talk about it and send cards they remind the person about it—as if I would ever forget that my baby died! I understand people are uncomfortable with the idea that I might cry in front of them, but the truth is that by listening to me or sending a card they make me know that at least they understand.

Unfortunately, very often the card does not get sent, the question does not get asked, and the listening does not happen. Instead, parents confront silence and discomfort from the world around them, learning quickly that they should not grieve, but if they must, they should do it alone and in silence.

SOCIAL, CULTURAL, ETHNIC, GENERATIONAL, AND RELIGIOUS/PHILOSOPHICAL BACKGROUND

Rando's (1984) discussion of these influences is quite cursory, stating that "differences due to culture, ethnic group, or religion/philosophy may help or hinder grief work" and that caregivers need to be aware of traditions that facilitate or hinder emotional expression (p. 55). My sample consisted primarily of white, middle-class, Canadian-born people; hence, my analysis focuses on the influence of dominant cultural ideals in modern, Western society rather than on differences that may exist between cultural groups.

Social influences

Modern Western society is highly mobile. People move for any number of reasons: in order to further educations, seek employment, or just because they feel their options might be better somewhere else. For a number of parents in the study, isolation occurred because they were far from traditional sources of social support, such as family, friends or a supportive, known religious community. For some parents, this isolation meant that their expectations of support were not high, and hence, they were less disappointed in the level of support they actually received. For other parents, the isolation they experienced was an additional burden in their mourning. One woman described her situation:

We had just moved out here, and although I was working, I really had not connected with anyone. Everyone was nice, and concerned, but I really did not feel like they knew me well enough for me to really be able to talk about what I was going through. It was a pretty bleak time.

For couples whose support networks are limited, the reliance on one another for support is increased that much more. Of course, the need for support from a partner does not necessarily improve the chances of it being available. Women who complained of feeling particularly isolated often complained that their partner's support has been inadequate as well.

One of the primary reasons parents gave for not attending a support group relates to this need for support from true intimates. Although parents were often not getting the level of support they needed from those they loved, they felt extremely ambivalent about seeking that support "from a roomful of strangers." Apparently, it is not just the right words that provide comfort, it is the right source that must provide those words. In a society that is highly mobile, where truly intimate relationships are few and far between, obtaining meaningful support is extremely difficult for many parents.

Cultural influences

In Chapter 3, I discussed some of the psychological impacts that occur when individuals subscribe to the larger cultural norms of stoicism and individualism. Not only individuals adhere to these values, even medical and "caring" institutions maintain values of individualism and stoicism. Frequently, women who were experiencing pregnancy complications before they lost their babies were told by physicians to go home and stay on bedrest, but they had to rely entirely on their own resources in order to implement those orders. Women's home and work situations often necessitated that they continue to prepare family meals, provide child care, and continue to go to work. Home care workers, home nurses, and sick-letters to employers would have enabled women to follow medical advice; however, these were seldom provided. Of course, many women were unable to adhere to medical regimes and were left feeling personally responsible and extremely guilty when they ended up losing their babies. Despite medical assurances that "these things just happen," they tortured themselves with a litany of "what-ifs": what if I had rested more, gone to the doctor sooner, stayed home from work, not run after my kids, not scrubbed the floor, not lifted up my other baby.

Following the deaths, and once mothers had been discharged from hospitals, both members of the couple were typically left to their own devices by the medical community. In interviewing hospital and mental health workers in the field of perinatal loss, it is clear that the primary reason for not contacting and following up on parents more aggressively stems from a desire not to force parents to become involved with caregivers or therapy. Despite the benign intentions, however, parents understand the nonintervention as a message to "take care of yourself, but do it quietly and without being a burden." As one woman said, "Once the big drama of trying to save the baby was over, they basically just dumped me."

Ethnic influences

Because of the limited nature of the sample, ethnic and subcultural influences are not readily identifiable in the data. There is a certain logic to this: Cultures that honor and validate perinatal loss would likely facilitate rather than complicate mourning; thus, members of these communities might be less motivated to share their stories of loss. Most research volunteers claimed they participated in this project so they could share their stories in hopes that others need not suffer as they did; parents who suffered less might not share this motivation. For example, I spoke with a Native American woman who told me that in her society a baby of any gestational age who dies will have a sacred naming ceremony in the community. Perhaps in communities like hers the pressure to go underground with one's grief is not so great, making the need to participate in studies like this one less compelling.

Generational influences

Western twentieth-century medicine has made tremendous advances in the field of reproductive health and new reproductive technologies. When parents in this sample learned about sex, the emphasis was on prevention of unwanted pregnancy rather than on the possibility of losing a desired pregnancy. In pregnancy, procedures such as amniocentesis further the illusion of choice; the procedure is performed to identify undesirable genetic traits in order to provide parents with the option of terminating the pregnancy. Likewise, ultrasounds are performed in order to identify muscoskeletal problems before children are born. Heart defects can be surgically repaired while the baby is still in utero. These procedures provide parents with a belief that medicine has made pregnancy and childbirth safe and predictable.

Parents expect medicine to be able to save their babies, to guarantee their choice, and to provide them with answers and reassurances when something unexpected does go wrong. Unfortunately, few parents in this sample were able to receive satisfactory answers as to why their babies did not survive. In past generations, perhaps the typical medical response that "these things just happen" might be more readily accepted. Today, however, with the larger cultural conception of medicine as infallible, parents who lack answers or identifiable medical causes are left believing that somehow they must be responsible for the loss. They tell themselves that they should have known their physician was incompetent or that they should have been more proactive with the medical profession in demanding what they needed. The modern understanding of medicine offers little room for parents to accept failure as a pregnancy outcome, leaving parents to assume their experience is both rare and unnatural.

Many parents described how little contact they had with perinatal loss prior to their own losses and yet how people just "seemed to come out of the woodwork" once it had occurred to them. Learning about the frequency of losses might be expected to reduce some of the self-blame attached to losing a child; however, it often offered cold comfort to parents. Typically, parents first heard about these other losses in response to telling people about their own child's death. To be told "Oh, that happened to an aunt of mine" in response to saying that your baby has died only serves to divert the conversation from the topic of personal loss into one of "general human interest." Again, parents find their need to talk deflected, and they are reduced to (often resentful) silence.

Religious/philosophical influences

When discussing psychological factors that complicate mourning, I described how parents' degree of affiliation with a religion can assist or inhibit them in receiving comfort from their churches. Having a strong faith can help an individual accept the answers provided by one's church; however, it is not only the individual's religiosity that can mediate the comfort religion can provide. Even parents who felt strongly about their church, who attended church regularly, who were involved in their church community, and who described themselves as very religious found their churches were woefully inadequate in providing support following their losses. Many described subtle pressures to conform to the dominant church ideology, often at the expense of their own feelings. One woman, a Mormon who has an active Calling in her church and who lives in a rural, Mormon community, described how difficult it has been for her to receive any validation for her feelings from members of her church and community:

It's just been really hard for me to talk about [my baby's] death with anybody connected to the Temple. Like, my best friend won't even listen to me—she told me she would never be sad, like when her mother dies, because she knows her Mom will just go to Heaven to wait for the rest of the family to come back up. So, if I do mention it, it's like I'm not following the faith.

This woman received a clear message from her religious community that to discuss any pain about her daughter's death would not be supported socially because in her religion a death is simply not interpreted as a loss. The silence that surrounds her grief tells her not only that it is inappropriate for her to speak of her loss, but that doing so amounts to an act of bad faith.

Even parents whose loss is understood as tragic by their church community find the support they receive is inappropriate. One woman described how her uncle, an Archbishop in the Catholic church, together with the Pope, prayed for her to have subsequent children:

Like, these great men of the Catholic church have *saintly* power...and so he and the Pope together go to the Shrine of Fertility in Rome or wherever it is and pray for my fertility! But that made me angry because he had never asked me if I wanted children—it was just something that was expected. It was just part of the doctrine, like you have to have babies, so he just took it upon himself to take the Pope up to pray for my uterus! Like, this is incredibly powerful—it's almost like going to God himself and saying, "Give her another baby." But I found that quite abusive actually.

This woman went on to describe the pressure she felt as a good Catholic to fulfill the destiny she had been set up for her. Instead of acknowledging her loss and honoring her pain, her church's message was "Yes, it's a shame, but your duty is to get on with another one as soon as possible." As is so often the case, the intentions behind this gesture were undoubtedly benign, but they acted to deny and minimize this woman's very real feelings of loss.

Another woman described how her priest attempted to provide solace within the public setting of a church service:

I was in the choir, and the priest began talking about the death of my baby. He said it was for the best because—who knows?—she might have grown up to marry outside of the faith! And I just had to stand there at the front of the church and listen to him! There's one for your report!

Again, even though this priest's intentions were probably benign, the message this woman received reflects societal norms that "these things happen for the best, and for reasons which we cannot understand." The comfort such statements provide is cold indeed.

Mourner's education, economic and occupation status

Rando (1984) tells us that "a lack of education, financial resources, or occupational skills will only magnify the stresses on the griever" (p. 55). In my study, I found support for this claim. I also noted a gendered quality to the influence of these factors on parental mourning.

Whether women are unpaid workers in the home, part-time or temporary workers in the workforce, or professional workers in the competitive world of business, their employment status often becomes contentious when they become pregnant. Difficulties at work become even more pressing when women's pregnancies become problematic. Both before their losses and following them, women commonly reported problems in getting the support they needed at work.

In our society, women often work in temporary or part-time positions. Temporary and part-time workers are typically not protected by unions, and consequently, they often experience occupational uncertainty. Several women in this study described the effect of their precarious position at work on their pregnancies and losses. One woman, a librarian, was newly hired and working in a temporary capacity when she became pregnant. She felt she had to hide her pregnancy or lose her job. Once problems began to arise, avoiding disclosure became increasingly difficult, and she began experiencing conflict with a supervisor who saw her as incompetent and unreliable.

A number of women in the sample worked in low paying jobs that provided no paid sick leave and no job security. Taking much-needed time from work meant risking lost income or perhaps even lost employment. For these women, structural circumstances inhibited their ability and willingness to take care of themselves before and following their losses. Women who were unable to do everything humanly possible to prevent pregnancy loss were left feeling guilty and responsible. Likewise, women who felt pushed back into the workplace after their loss often wished they could have taken more time to process their grief.

Even women who were in solid, unionized or professional positions experienced problems at work once they became pregnant. One participant, a female member of a military combat troop, felt that she had to prove herself to her male coworkers, despite problems with bleeding, nausea and dehydration throughout the entire 5 months of her pregnancy. At the time, there was no policy to put pregnant soldiers on light duty, so she went on field exercises along with the other members of her unit and received no special consideration for her condition. As a woman in a man's world, when she asked for time off or assistance in carrying her field gear, her demands were seen as an additional burden to be borne by her male coworkers and constituted "proof" that women should not be in the military. Another woman, a paramedic, reported being sidelined in her work when she became pregnant, and she felt that her coworkers resented her pregnancy because it increased their workload. Again, when problems arose, she felt a need to downplay them rather than risk further friction at work. In a society that merely tolerates pregnant women in the workplace, pregnant women with problems are treated with even less sympathy. Again, the need to keep things smooth at work can often interfere with their ability to do all they can to maintain their pregnancies.

A final, and common, occupational status for women is that of an unpaid worker in the home. Almost half of the women in my study were stay-at-home parents at the time of their losses. These women's labor was not paid, so the issue of compensation or assistance during problem pregnancies and recoveries never even came up. Again, real support in the form of monetary compensation to pay for help in the home or physical assistance to replace their labor in the home was simply not available. Women in this position, too, were faced with difficult choices between doing their job at home or taking care of their pregnancies and, later, accommodating their grief.

Funerary or memorial rites

The absence of rituals that "promote realization and confirmation of the loss, assist in the expression of affect and memories, and offer social support to the bereaved" can be extremely detrimental to the grief process (Rando, 1984, p. 55). Unfortunately, funeral rituals are only tentatively suggested and are often even actively discouraged by hospitals, families, and friends. In many cases, parents themselves choose not to observe rituals at the time of their loss.

The one thing that parents in this study wished for is that they had more time with their babies. In the hospital, babies are generally handed to parents, but parents are given clear messages about what behaviors are appropriate. Frequently, mothers were warned not to hold their babies too long because the warmth of the mothers' bodies would accelerate the deterioration of their babies' bodies. Parents were discouraged from repeated contact, being warned that their babies might not look great after the first viewing because of skin slippage. Parents who requested permission to take their babies home were, with one notable exception, refused. The general message is that "you should say goodbye, but there are strict limits on where you can do it and how long it should take you."

Parents frequently describe how difficult it was for them to actually leave the hospital without a baby in their arms. To leave without the baby is to abandon the child, often to a precarious fate. One couple's baby was lost by the hospital, who sent the funeral director away empty-handed when he came to claim the body. As the parents were too hysterical to cope, their physician acted as advocate, located the body, made the proper transfer arrangements with the funeral home, and resolved the problem. Nonetheless, this couple's feelings of distrust in leaving the baby's body to hospital care were borne out.

Leaving the babies in the hospital is even more distressing for parents who opt not to have a funeral. At the time, parents make these decisions based on hospital advice—it seems that they are doing the correct thing. Later, they express misgivings, knowing they have relinquished their only opportunity to care for their children and that they have left them in the care of strangers. Several women described how they had wanted to go back to the hospital after leaving, just to have one more look at their babies, and yet they knew that the body would not be there if they asked. There is an unspoken, but dread, knowledge for these parents that their babies have ended up in a hospital incinerator, just another piece of medical waste. There are simply no second chances for these parents—they must decide within a few hours of losing their child what they will do, and once those decisions are made, they must live with them forever. The hospital's need to move patients through quickly, to avoid physical deterioration of the corpse, to not have babies' bodies taking up space in freezers for a week or two until parents can collect their thoughts override the human need of people in shock to take time, to provide what little love they can, and to decide wisely what must be done.

For parents, the struggle to take a baby home or to dress the baby after an autopsy has been performed or to hold the baby through the night despite physical deterioration represents the only opportunity they will have to physically care for their lost child. The unspoken fear of medical practitioners is that this desire to care for a child is precariously close to pathological behavior: perhaps parents might never return the body, might never let go of their child, might see the autopsy scars, might hold the baby until the flesh does begin to rot. The message to parents is that wanting to provide that care, wanting to ensure that their babies have been treated respectfully by the pathology department, or wanting to keep the baby safely at home until going to the funeral parlor is strange and dangerous. In fact, to many parents, wanting to protect their child is the most natural thing they can imagine.

Parents who may have never had contact with a death, who are not prepared for one, and who have never considered that they might need to plan and pay for their baby's funeral are particularly vulnerable to the message hospitals give that this is an event to get through quickly and to put behind them just as quickly. Many expressed regrets at the time of our interviews that they had not received more instruction or guidance throughout their decision-making process.

The point is, despite the rhetoric of hospitals that they do not want to push parents or direct their decision-making, hospitals are not neutral in the messages they send to parents. Parents are not told they **should** have a funeral, nor are they told they **should** get a birth and death certificate issued, nor are they told they **should** have an autopsy, nor are they told they **should** spend as much time as possible holding, loving and saying goodbye to their babies. They are, however, told that they **should not** hold the baby too long, that they **should not** take too long to decide what to do about the body, that they **should not** want to take the baby home, look at its autopsy scars, or expect to come back and be able to change their minds later. The messages parents receive are decidedly mixed and not entirely helpful.

Funeral homes, too, contribute to messages that certain behaviors are acceptable, and others are beyond decency. One woman ran into resistance from the Funeral Director when she asked to dress her own baby. She explains:

> We wanted to dress her, and the director said, "You don't want to see your baby after the autopsy," and he insisted on dressing her before he'd let us hold her. I mean, this baby had been in my body dead—it did not gross me out that she was dead. So I took her hat and all the clothes off her and looked at what they had done anyway. I mean, I needed to know that they had not mutilated her and left her there.

Later, just before the funeral, it was again necessary for her to assert herself in order to see her baby one last time:

> The [funeral director] said, "There's been skin slippage, you understand what that is?" He was very concerned that we couldn't deal with this. And I said, "Yes." I was very *happy* that I was going to see her again, and I'm sure he thought I was really strange to be so eager to see her. And he let us in, and it was almost like he did not want to leave, like he was afraid we might break down. And finally my

husband had to ask him for some time alone with her. And even then, he hung around.

For this couple, dressing their baby, holding her, talking to her, and saying goodbye one final time were very strong desires. They knew what they wanted and were willing to assert their needs despite resistance and discouragement from professionals. For most parents, however, the knowledge of what they want to do for their children is not this clear, and they only understand what they want when it is much too late. It is simply too much for such parents to resist the social messages of what is "appropriate" or to demand that events be conducted according to their own hearts rather than according to prevailing norms about how a baby's death **should** be handled.

Parents' ability to honor the death was also curtailed by finances. For many parents, the decision not to have a funeral was reached because of financial constraints. Even for parents who did opt for a funeral, money was a factor. One woman described her feelings after choosing an inexpensive coffin for her baby:

> When I went to the funeral home, they showed us a number of coffins, and some of them were beautiful—all lace and satin-lined. But we ended up taking this styrofoam thing—it really looked almost like a cooler. I really felt bad about that, but that was all we could afford, and we weren't allowed to make something ourselves. It really hurt me to see her in that thing.

The symbolism of the styrofoam container was not lost on this woman: This is a disposable container for a disposable death. That she was unable to do more for her child remains a source of pain.

Involvement in the legal system

Rando (1993) discusses the complicating influences of the legal system, for example, in cases of murder where survivors must negotiate legal and judicial systems that are additional sources of frustration and pain (pp. 548–549). In the case of perinatal loss, the juncture between parents' private grief experiences and legal structures is of interest not because those systems are intrusive, but rather because they are so conspicuously absent.

The legal system is typically a recurring part of modern life. In prenuptial agreements, in divorce, in buying a home, in handling a death, lawyers are often involved in our major life passages. They rarely come into play in the death of a baby, emphasizing the ambiguous status of a perinatal death.

Insurance companies, too, are generally involved in an illness or death, yet they are conspicuous by their absence at perinatal deaths. Those parents who did check with insurance companies were told that their employee or private insurance plans would not cover any costs attached to the death—the baby has never lived, so the life has never been insured. This is the quintessential bureaucratic form of the message "you cannot lose what you never had," and it adds to the chorus of silence that parents consistently hear—their loss is simply not important enough to discuss or to put down on paper. As discussed in the Chapter 3, hospitals also contribute to the bureaucratic silence surrounding perinatal death by discouraging parents from processing birth and death certificates and claiming that this omission is an act of generosity. In fact, many parents see this as yet another message that this was not "really" a life and, hence, not "really" a death.

Amount of time since the death

Our culture holds an expectation that as life and time go on feelings of emptiness and loss will necessarily abate. This assumption is not always true as grief can be triggered anew, and with surprising ferocity, by events that remind mourners of their loss.

The nature of an anticipated relationship with a child is intertwined with many such triggers. A child will pass through a long litany of "firsts"; many of our religious and secular holidays are child-centered; almost any involvement with family or extended family will involve children; and the process of birth, of life itself can act as a reminder of opportunities lost. Thus, parents are often subject to STUGS caused by encountering reminders of the child who was to be. Christmas, Easter, Mother's Day, anniversary dates, beginnings of school years, births within the immediate and extended family, watching other children (either one's own or those of family and friends) go through developmental milestones, hearing snatches of music that were popular when one was pregnant, seeing baby clothing in a store, hearing of a dear friend's (successful or unsuccessful) pregnancy, there are so many possibilities for triggering grief anew. Therefore, although the day-to-day pain of losing a baby might abate as time passes, there is always that possibility for renewed grief lurking in seemingly innocent and joyous places.

There is a particular pain to being surrounded by life and its celebration while feeling alone and alien in one's pain. One woman described her feelings during a baby shower she was hosting for a friend:

> I looked around, and everyone who was in the room had either just had a baby or was pregnant, and you can guess what the conversation

was. I just stood there and thought, "I have nothing to contribute here." I really did not want to stay, but it was my place, and where was I gonna go? I felt so trapped.

This woman's pain was made more poignant by being juxtaposed against the joy shared by her friends and family in "normal" life events. Parents often find themselves in settings like this, where what others take for granted as a normal, joyous entitlement is contrasted with their own knowledge of those things as fleeting, elusive and painful. They also have learned that to express their sorrow at such times is not only inappropriate, but often is met with statements that clearly tell them not to "keep bringing that up again."

SOCIAL AND PSYCHOLOGICAL FACTORS—CONCLUSIONS

Rando presents a comprehensive typology of social and psychological factors that can enhance or complicate mourning. From talking to parents, it is clear that the possibility for complicated mourning exists in every psychological and social category of Rando's typology. In fact, because the possibilities for complications are so extensive, it is likely that any parent who has lost a child to perinatal death is at risk for at least some complications in resolving their grief.

Chapter 5
Giving Death: The Body and Perinatal Loss

Rando (1993) offers a comprehensive typology of physiological factors that potentially contribute to complicated mourning. The physiological influences she describes refer to the state of the mourner and how that state affects the coping abilities needed to recover from a loss: for example, the influence of drugs and alcohol on mourners; the effects of nutrition on coping abilities; the amount of rest and sleep mourners get; the amount of exercise mourners get; and how the mourners' general physical health can aid or inhibit their grief resolution (Rando, 1993, p. 32). In perinatal death, these influences are important, but more important, the mourner's body is itself typically the site of the death. Thus, parents not only are recovering from the death of another, but mothers are recovering from the death as it occurs *within* them. In this sense, mothers have a physical experience of death unlike that of most mourners, and their bodies complicate mourning in ways that are unique to perinatal loss.

EXERCISE

In her discussion, Rando (1984, p. 57) explains that exercise is beneficial for mourners as it enhances the mourner's health, contributing to the mourner's ability to resolve grief. In addition, exercise provides an emotional release that facilitates the mourning process. In my study, women who were homebound or parents who were working and raising a family were constrained by time from participating in physical exercise. Nonetheless, even if parents did have the time to exercise or engage in hobbies, they frequently described simply not wanting to have to face others, of not wanting to have to pretend that they were carefree and fully alive. Because so often their social interactions were nonvalidating and painful, they chose to stay home and hibernate rather than face the world. The risk in this type of hibernation is that parents' withdrawal isolates them further, cutting them off from any support or enjoyment that might be available to them.

DRUGS AND SEDATIVES

According to Rando (1984), the negative effects of psychopharmacological agents may outweigh their usefulness in numbing the pain. She points out that mourners who are sedated for the funeral, for example, may miss that opportunity to say goodbye (Rando, 1984, p. 55). For mothers, who are typically anaesthetized and sedated during the births of children who are not expected to survive, the opportunity to say goodbye is not all that is lost: the opportunity to say hello is also taken away.

The mothers in my sample were often encouraged by medical personnel to numb themselves during labor and delivery. The rationale for heavy medication during labor was that since nothing further could go wrong with the delivery women might as well be anaesthetized as much as possible—that being medically numb would help them to remain emotionally numb. Unfortunately, the emotional numbness that drugs induce often works to hamper women's ability to be fully present at the only opportunity they will have to know and care for their child. Women suffer from a profound sense of lost opportunity as a direct result of this seemingly benign anaesthetization. Once the drugs wear off, once the day has passed, it is often far too late to rescind decisions made or to reclaim bodies that may already be disposed of. The long-term pain women live with is often worsened by regrets that are a direct result of being medicated during and immediately following the loss.

Medical intentions of minimizing women's emotions through drugs persist long after the delivery has occurred. Several women spoke of seeing their physicians following the loss and having their feelings passed off as something that should have disappeared by then. One woman explains:

About a year after our last baby died, I went to my physician and said, "I just cannot seem to get back on track, like, I'm still really feeling down and can't get rid of this weight," and all this other stuff. And she basically just wrote me a prescription for Prozac and told me to get over it.

Another woman described being referred to a psychiatrist by her family doctor, when all she really wanted was to talk to someone who knew her situation and who would sympathize. This woman never did make the psychiatric appointment, saying, "I knew all he'd do is write me a prescription, and that was only going to make things worse." These women are clearly being told that their grief is pathological and that a pill will fix them up and take away the pain. In fact, nothing so simple will take away the pain. The one thing that women do need—to talk about their loss, to have it taken seriously, to hear that what they feel is legitimate—is something that the medical community is, apparently, not prepared to offer. Further, by writing a prescription for psychoactive substances, physicians respond to women's need to talk as though that need itself is a sickness.

NUTRITION

Rando (1984, p. 56) describes loss of appetite as a common response to a loss and encourages caregivers to ensure that mourners receive adequate nutrition so they will have the energy to work through their grief. In my sample, a number of women had just the opposite problem, actually gaining weight after their loss. This additional weight gain was a source of pain for these women, who not only lost their babies, but lost their former selves under a layer of protective fat. The additional weight struck women as yet another failure of their bodies to do what is right and desirable for a woman in this culture. One woman explains:

I have difficulty with pregnancy, and I have difficulty with birth. And of course, I'm—I've become a yo-yo dieter. I've never been happy with my body, and so I just feel more angry at it. It's just another thing that by body can't do, so my weight is very much an issue for me.

The cultural ideal of the thin, sexual woman acts to reinforce for these women that their bodies are a site of betrayal. They are not capable of mothering. They are not attractively slender. They are failures.

Poor nutrition can be problematic, too, for women who are overwhelmed by their grief. Several women discussed how, after their loss, they were so incompetent that they could not perform simple tasks. Their homes were a mess, half the time the kids did not get fed on schedule, and they just "let themselves go." Typically, they "let themselves go" in solitude because home-workers were never assigned from the hospital to check up on them, grand-mothers who typically might help out in the home after the birth of a living child often failed to see the need for assistance once the baby died, community members did not provide food and meals as so often happens when a "real" birth or death occurs, and husbands returned to work swiftly after the loss. When a baby lives, these supports are more frequently available to post-partum mothers. The message is that without a baby to care for women do not need public health nurse visits, their own mothers' assistance, community support, or paternal support in the home.

REST AND SLEEP

Rando (1984, p. 56) cites a lack of sleep as detrimental to the resources a mourner can bring to the recovery process, suggesting medication if the problem becomes too severe. Almost all the mothers in the sample reported insomnia, while fathers seldom mentioned experiencing this problem. In part, this may reflect the women's positions in the homes following their loss, where they are often isolated and understimulated. They wander around the house, nap, and are generally listless. With days that undertax them, their nights are often interrupted with dreams of the baby, by hearing cries in the night, by feeling kicks that are no longer "real." Women's bodies become a stage where a lot of unspoken grief is acted out. And much of that action occurs at night, when nothing else exists to distract them. The result is a cycle of long, weary days and long, tortured nights. Because only women seem to suffer from these late-night awakenings, insomnia itself is a symptom that can work to drive a wedge between partners. Women describe lying awake, crying, or quietly obsessing on the loss and feeling a tremendous resentment against their seemingly placid, sleeping partners.

PHYSICAL HEALTH

When Rando (1984, p. 57) discusses physical health and mourning, it is simply to point out that grief itself takes a toll on the mourner's well-being. She admonishes caregivers to watch for physical symptoms that might accompany grief and treat them appropriately so as to facilitate the grief process. Like any mourner, parents who suffer perinatal loss may also experience stresses on their well-being from the grief itself. In perinatal loss, however, there are other physical influences that go beyond proper diet, rest, exercise and physical health and any secondary physical illnesses that might arise to inhibit the grief process. For women who have lost a baby to peri- natal death, the death occurs within the context of physical changes that accompany any pregnancy, labor and delivery. Thus, physical health is a par- ticularly salient influence on women's ability to resolve their grief.

Besides dealing with the death of another person, women are recovering from childbirth. A few women in this study had postpartum infections and low blood levels as a result of difficult birth experiences. Even women who had "normal" deliveries had physical problems to contend with following the death: they were tired and were subject to mood swings that were (perhaps inappropriately) attributed by themselves and others to be the result of the hormone changes that normally accompany childbirth. Women's bodies change once they deliver their babies, whether the baby lives or dies. Their stomachs become flatter, they bleed, and their breasts fill with milk. Normally, these physical symptoms are met with pleasure: the flattened stomach is a sign for mothers that they are returning to normal; the bleed- ing is a symptom of their fertility; the lactation is a sign of their ability to nurture; the birth itself becomes a symbol of their passage to motherhood. For women whose babies die, however, normal postpartum symptoms can be extremely painful.

The flattened stomach is not merely a sign that one has returned to nor- mal, but that one is empty. Many women described how unreal their bodies looked and felt to them after the loss. One woman described how seeing herself in a mirror for the first time after her loss was almost like receiving a physical blow—her own image served as irrefutable proof of her loss.

Almost all of the women in the sample had their breasts fill with milk after the baby was born. For some women, their milk came as confirmation that something really had happened to them, that they had indeed been pregnant and lost a child. For others, lactation acted as an unanticipated reminder of what they had lost. Perhaps because the actual birth experiences so often unfolded in a blur of activity and medication, this physical reminder that a birth had occurred was often experienced as a shock, and women are not typically coached to expect lactation. One woman in the sample was a physician, and even she had not "expected a woman to lactate so early in pregnancy." Full breasts, particularly when not emptied regularly through breastfeeding, can be extremely painful. The painfully full breasts, the post- partum mood swings, the fatigue of childbirth, the emptiness, all present a physical constellation of "ills" that act to confront and remind women of their loss. One woman describes how her body felt after the loss:

After a day or two my milk came in—it was a really hard time. Having my milk come in was really, really hard. And I remember feeling sort of flattened for a while. I kept feeling like I'd left something behind, like I'd forgotten something, or I was missing something in the hospital.

The physical pain of lactation and the physical feeling of emptiness are often accompanied by a physical yearning. Women spoke of literally feeling that both their stomachs and their arms were empty and aching. It is as if women's bodies tell them what has happened even if they themselves might wish to push it aside.

In many cases, the physical changes that are so painful to women may not even be noticeable to others. For women who are not yet really showing their pregnancies or who may simply look like they have put on a few pounds, a flatter stomach may be perceived by others as a weight loss. A number of women described painful interactions with coworkers or more distant acquaintances where they had not only to explain their loss, but had to explain that they had even been pregnant. An enormous life event to these women, the loss is not even noteworthy to others.

Sometimes, although the woman feels empty, she may not look that different from her pregnant self. A woman who returned to work immediately after her loss explains:

> I was working in a fairly visible position, and not everybody had heard and I still, I guess, looked pregnant when I got back. And one fellow who was really nice said, "How's 'Junior' doing?" and I just couldn't handle it. And I'm sure four or five people came in and asked how the baby was doing.

For this woman, the pain of dealing with her loss was compounded by having to explain her loss again and again to people around her who did not even notice it. It is extremely painful to have something so pivotal seem trivial to others, but the simple fact is that for many of those others the loss is not even physically (let alone emotionally) comprehended.

The site of the loss, and of the life that preceded it, is in women's bodies. This can present problems, even within couples. Here, one woman poignantly describes the role that physically carrying a child played in contrasting her grief with her husband's:

> [My husband]...does not respond in the same way as I do. Simply because he did not know my daughter like I knew her. She lived inside

of me, not him. You know, he could feel her move but it was different—put his hand on my tummy or whatever—so his loss is for the loss of what could have been. It wasn't for me—it was more—it was the loss of what *was*. She was inside me, and she was very much my baby before she was born. So I lost *somebody*. I feel like I knew her.

The physical intimacy a pregnant woman shares with her child, beginning long before birth, binds her to that child in a way that is simply, physically impossible for another human to share. In this way, her physical connection to the dead child sets her apart from everyone else, even those who share the loss.

A SPECIAL KIND OF PAIN

For many of the women in this study, the most painful memory they have is the body memory of giving birth. Frequently, female participants who remained composed throughout the rest of their interviews broke down when actually describing the births of their children. In a sense, women are not merely people who lose someone they love, they physically participate in the loss. Their bodies are the sites of a terrible trauma—the sensations of the child's birth and death are one and are precipitated by often painful labor:

And I went through the birthing process, and I could feel her shoulders and her head and her arms—I could feel her toenails as she passed out of me—I could feel her being born. And I knew that, as she was being born, she was dying.

The sensation of giving birth seems to remain, like a brand, in women's skin. They felt it. They participated in it. It is a horror that will not wash away, no matter how much time passes. Another woman describes her feelings about the birth:

I think the very, very hardest part was when the baby came out. And every other time, you know, you have that—yelling, you know, the crying, and you're just so excited, and you're just so—elated. And just to see this limp, little body...(crying)...and the room was just so silent.

The act of giving birth, the experience of delivering, becomes an act of violence, a moment of trauma. It is a memory to be relived again and again, to be reexperienced not only as a visual image or a series of sounds and smells, but as an actual physical sensation: "I *felt* it. It happened, and it happened in *me.*" This, perhaps more than any other thing, is a source of mothers' guilt. The frequent accounts women gave of refusing to push during labor or of waiting until the very last moment to go to the hospital are representative of their futile efforts **not** to participate in the deaths of their children, and yet, cruelly, they have no choice. The baby must be born, and this can only happen with the mother's cooperation.

Fathers also experience the death as a personal trauma, not because it occurs in their bodies or because they physically experience trauma of their own, but because they are inevitably witnesses to the death. The present day practice in obstetrics is to encourage fathers to attend births. This practice carries over into births that are not expected to go well. Fathers in this study were not present at caesarean sections; however, they generally attended vaginal births, which comprised the majority of births in this study. The physical presence and involvement of fathers as labor coaches and as emotional supports meant that they, too, actively participated in the deaths of their children.

Their role as "assistant" or as "pillar of strength" to mothers in labor can act to exacerbate men's feelings of helplessness, and it highlights the fact that their role as parent and as mourner is ancillary to the mother's. Men described how difficult it was for them to watch their wives go through the pain and risk of labor knowing or suspecting what the outcome would be. Their worries were not only for their children, but for their wives as well. Their feelings were not only sorrow or worry, but impotence and horror at watching events unfold before their eyes.

Conclusion

The physical factors that can influence perinatal mourning, like the social and psychological factors, all represent areas that presented difficulties for parents who are coping with perinatal loss. As I discussed earlier, the social problems parents experience interact with their psychological interpretations of the situation to create complications in grief resolution. Likewise, the physical symptoms parents deal with are influenced by social and psychological factors. Swollen breasts are more than a physical fact for women who have delivered a dead child—reaction to the swelling is influenced by social expectations and psychological interpretations. The social fact of being unprepared by medicine for lactation and the psychological impact of women's interpretation of lactation as another indicator of failed motherhood are typical of the complex interplay that occurs between social, psychological and physical factors for bereaved parents. Their bodies, their beliefs and attitudes, their interactions and social experiences all work to create a particularly complex maze to be negotiated in grief resolution. Nonetheless, parents do manage, in extremely creative ways, to negotiate that maze.

Chapter 6
Creating Meaning, Experiencing Growth

In previous chapters, I discussed the influences of psychological, social and physiological factors on parental grief. I also argued that all three categories work interactively to complicate mourning, and a parent's psychological beliefs may accentuate or counter the impact of social messages and can likewise affect their physical symptoms. For example, the woman who interprets her breastmilk as a reminder of failed womanhood will have a different experience of that symptom than the woman who interprets it as a confirmation that indeed her child has lived and died. I believe the parents who are most adaptive in their grief resolution are those who are able to go beyond the traditional norms of perinatal mourning that society imposes on them. They interpret or respond to their experiences in a way that I will describe as postmodern. The following story encompasses the difference between one woman's traditional and postmodern experiences of perinatal loss:

> One woman who contributed to my study had a stillborn daughter in 1957. Her loss experience was highly structured; there was a funeral and an autopsy, but almost immediately following the loss, the doors were closed—seemingly forever—on the subject of her dead child. She recalled her experience as something she never really attempted to challenge. She learned quickly to put her losses behind her, at least in

a conscious way. Twenty-three years later, her 26-year-old son was senselessly killed by a drunk driver, and she found this death compelled her to reassess her feelings around the earlier one. In the intervening years, the culture in which she lives has changed enough to accommodate her desire to reexplore and reexperience the older loss. The church she belongs to is the same one in which, 29 years ago, the priest declared from his pulpit that the baby's death was God's way of avoiding a marriage outside the faith. It now houses a lay ministry to the bereaved, where she has been encouraged to reclaim the death of her child and to honor her loss all these years later. Her need to grieve is now accepted as healthy, and her methods of doing so are encouraged to be personally meaningful.

This woman's early experience is typical of what I will call traditional norms of perinatal mourning. In losing a child to perinatal loss, she found her personal experiences were in conflict with prevailing norms and traditions regarding mourning, yet she had little choice but to adhere to her society's standards for mourning a perinatal loss. She assimilated these norms so well that they constrained her private experiences of grief; she herself believed she had "put the death behind her." In her earlier experience, it was understood by all parties that there was a "right" and "normal" way to deal with stillbirth or perinatal loss, and so the experience was lived, at least consciously, as it "should" have been.

This woman's recent experience of grief has been radically different in that the "shoulds" that surround her grief resolution are now offered as options, to be used as she sees fit. This approach is postmodern in that it understands that personal solutions are indeed the only ones that can truly resonate (Bauman, 1993, p. 34). Hence, this woman has been able to say and do what she needs to in order to process her grief, and it is her interpretation of the loss that has guided the response and understanding of those around her. It is a direct reversal of the traditional flow of norms. When she adhered to a traditional style of mourning, she followed the guidelines that were imposed from her society; in postmodernity, she has selected those rituals and interpretations that she finds suitable, has translated them to fit her personal situation, and has enacted them within her society. Through her enactments, she informs her world about what it is that she finds appropriate and what, in turn, it is that she needs from that world in order to best satisfy her particular needs.

THE SIX "R's" OF MOURNING

In the preceding chapters, I described how parents' private experiences of grief frequently came into conflict with public norms and standards surrounding perinatal loss. In this chapter, I explore how parents used a postmodern approach to claim their losses as real and to create their own paths to healing. I use Rando's (1993) typology of six "R" processes necessary for resolving mourning to organize my analysis. These six "R" processes are:

1. Recognize the loss
   •Acknowledge the death
   •Understand the death
2. React to the separation
   •Experience the pain
   •Feel, identify, accept and give some form of expression to all the psychological reactions to the loss
   •Identify and mourn secondary losses
3. Recollect and reexperience the deceased and the relationship
   •Review and remember realistically
   •Revive and reexperience the feelings
4. Relinquish the old attachments to the deceased and the old assumptive world
5. Readjust to move adaptively into the new world without forgetting the old
   •Revise the assumptive world
   •Develop a new relationship with the deceased
   •Adopt new ways of being in the world
   •Form a new identity
6. Reinvest

I explore each of these processes, briefly describing some of the structural blocks to grief resolution and then some of the creative strategies parents employed in overcoming those blocks. Again, not everyone in this study had experienced all of these processes, and many described how they often thought they had "done with grieving" only to be forced by some unanticipated turn of events to confront a new aspect of their grief. Thus, the examples I offer below represent ways of dealing with and growing through perinatal loss, but they should not be understood as a linear description of "how perinatal grief is resolved." The process is much more complex than that, occurring piecemeal, often with one aspect presenting itself repeatedly or preceding another out of turn.

RECOGNIZE THE LOSS

There are two elements in recognizing any loss. First, mourners must acknowledge the reality of the death and its irreversibility so that they can begin to grieve. Second, mourners must understand the facts and circumstances that surround the death so that they will not be overwhelmed with questioning what could have been (Rando, 1993, pp. 43–44).

Acknowledge the death

If the mourner does not admit the death occurred, he/she is then able to construe the loss as temporary. For all mourners, it is a natural urge to avoid confronting death. Thus, it is critical that mourners be confronted by sufficient evidence of the death so that they are not able to postpone or rationalize away their grief. This is why, for example, recovering the body of a loved one after an accident is so critical (Rando, 1993, p. 50).

Recognizing or admitting that the child is dead is often difficult for parents with perinatal losses. I described earlier how parents often did not acknowledge the death as real until labor was over and they were faced with irrefutable evidence of the death in the form of the baby's corpse. Parents in this study experienced particular difficulties in understanding that a death really had occurred as they often did not see or hold the baby's body and could not take time to discuss the loss as it was occurring. The speed, often medically induced, of many women's labor meant that parents had little time to absorb what was happening to them, while the drugs that mothers are encouraged to take often resulted in reducing the women's ability to understand and accept the death.

There were a few couples in my study who had the opportunity to fully acknowledge the loss as it was happening. Two things facilitated this process: first, the hospital took on a directive role in guiding parents to resources they would need; and second, time was granted to parents to begin the decision-making and mourning process. Hospital guidance in perinatal loss has been significantly altered because of parent lobbying and education. In this sense, the hospitals have learned from parents who have refused to accept the status quo how to encourage parents to be flexible and creative in their decision making about perinatal loss. Despite glitches due to budget cuts and staff shortages, hospitals have attempted to become more flexible.

Granting parents time to get used to the death prior to delivering the baby occurred primarily because parents themselves demanded it. Two couples in this study were actually able to go home from the hospital before delivering their babies, in both instances because the parents themselves insisted on taking that time. Rather than being corralled into a quick delivery and an accelerated decision-making process, these parents were able to go home and talk about what was happening to them and how they intended to respond to their new reality. Granting parents time once problems are first understood is not always possible for medical reasons; however, when the baby was already dead and the mother was not at immediate risk, those extra few hours really did seem to make a difference.

One couple was able to ask for what they needed throughout their experience, but they were only able to get it because their doctor was unusually understanding. The woman provides the following example of how her struggles unfolded:

> We got back to the room and waited for the findings from the ultrasound. And he finally called and said the baby had died, and then my doctor came up to the hospital. And they wanted to keep me overnight. And I did not want to stay. I wanted to go home. So she finally agreed. She sent me home and made me promise to come in—they'd induce me in the morning.

It was only because her physician was willing to vouch for her that she was discharged for the night. During that night, this couple held each other and cried. They chose a name for their son and discussed funeral and baptismal arrangements. They had been given a book by the nursing staff that guided them in their decision making and were able to use it as a beginning point for their own process. By the time they returned to the hospital the next day, they were no longer living in fierce hopes that a miracle would occur but had begun to understand that what they would do in the next few hours and days would be the only opportunity they would have to care for and express their feelings to their son. This understanding guided their postloss behavior and provided a solid foundation for working through their grieving process.

The role of the hospital in providing parents with direction and time cannot be underestimated; parents who had time, who were given clear guidance on what they would want to consider and what they might regret doing or not doing were generally much more accepting of the losses they suffered. Holding the baby, touching it, counting its fingers and toes, knowing its sex are all ways of acknowledging both the life and the death of a newborn baby. Without this closure, it seems to be very difficult for parents to challenge the disbelief and denial that "naturally" accompanies sudden, unexpected death (Rando, 1993, p. 44). One woman, in a letter to her labor nurse, poignantly describes what that guidance meant to her during her few hours with her daughter:

Dear Rita,

It was a week ago today that M. was delivered; and so many times since then, I have thought of you and what a difference it made to me to have you there....when I held her and examined her. You gave me time and space to do it alone—but also shared her with us. Your observations about her specifically—pointing out the beginning of hair or marvelling with me at the length of her fingers—and your comments about what she shared with others still-born—allowed me to know her as my own child, and accept her as one who died.

Compare the guidance this woman received from her delivery nurse to the woman whose child was held for her at arms' length, without any encouragement to hold or cuddle the child, then whisked away after a few silent seconds with the comment "Okay, well that's enough now." The feeling rules that Rita conveyed were able to accommodate the child as an individual, as a life to be honored and acknowledged, and they encouraged the mother to explore her own feelings and needs surrounding the loss from the very beginning. The feeling rules the other mother encountered told her that the death was not worth a great deal of time or consideration and that to expect accommodation and understanding, even from a professional, would be asking too much.

Happily, many parents in this sample whose losses were within the last 2 or 3 years did not have painful and counterproductive experiences with medical staff. Parent support groups have been active in informing hospital workers about what they and other parents who suffer a loss might need to consider, be advised of and be encouraged to do. Many of these suggestions have become hospital protocol and include being encouraged to hold, touch, see, and say goodbye to the dead child. Parents described some of their most tender memories in the hospital: bathing their babies, dressing them, holding them, having them baptized. One woman describes her baby's first moments:

I delivered him, and right away [my husband's] pastor baptized him for us. And my cousin, who's a nurse, had brought her camera, and she took a whole roll of film for us with our son. Which I'm incredibly grateful that we have that memory. And then [my husband] bathed him, and we took him back to the room, and we just held him that night.

Although this woman is describing the birth of a stillborn child, the description could just as easily be of a live birth. There is a certain solemn joy present in her description of the occasion, an acknowledgment that something monumental has occurred, that a life has happened and requires celebration. In effect, these parents transformed traditional rituals of birth to create their own, postmodern rituals for their child's death.

There were a few parents in this sample who were able to demand time to understand their loss on their own terms, despite social cues from medical personnel to the contrary. One woman actually managed to take her baby's body home with her after the birth. She describes how this occurred and what taking him home accomplished for her:

> Yup, we asked to be able to take him. There were some complications because the lab did not want us to take him, and the obstetrician did not want us to take him because I guess it's a health risk, but I mean we took him. We had all the funeral arrangements made before that point, so they were fairly confident that we were gonna be okay. And it was like all of those steps were a part of the healing.

This couple, the same couple who had been able to go home for a night before having labor induced, had a fortunate ally in their family physician, who was willing to vouch for her patients in the face of the hospital's resistance. It is rare, however, that parents are actually permitted to bring their baby home. One father in my study, acknowledging how painful it would be for his wife to come home without a baby, tells the following story:

> I do not know if I had been told ahead of time or if I just thought of it, but I had to get something to her so she did not leave empty-handed. My wife collects stuffed animals, so I brought her a plush german shepherd puppy she wanted. We had passed it up a couple of times because of the price. It wasn't the same as having a baby to take home, but it was a memory that we have. And I did that for both kids. So you do not have to leave empty-handed. (crying) So we never really forget them.

This couple lost two children, only saw and held their second son, and received no photographs or other artifacts from the hospitals for either child. The stuffed animals represent the sole physical evidence they have that their children lived and died. They also represent a very creative response to a very real dilemma.

Understand the death

Rando (1993) states that "without a context for understanding a loved one's death or some sort of rationale for it, a mourner tends to become anxious and confused, wondering about what happened to her loved one" (p. 47). Thus, without a reason for the death, there are constant questions that hamper mourning. A frustrating and disturbing aspect of perinatal loss is the lack of answers medicine is able to provide. Very few parents in this study were able to receive satisfactory answers from the medical community as to why their babies died. Those who did have a cause diagnosed, generally uterine malformation, were often able to have those problems corrected and go on to have successful subsequent pregnancies. For parents who were less fortunate, unanswered questions often acted as stumbling blocks to their healing. Parents whose losses "just happened" unfortunately have few choices in addressing those unanswered questions. Many parents did not have autopsies at the time because they were often discouraged from proceeding with an autopsy by physicians who advised them that in all likelihood nothing would be found.

In some cases, the attending physician seemed to contribute to, or sometimes even be responsible for, the death. In these instances, the silence and denial of the medical system itself often blocks the parents' understanding of the death. When physicians do have a hand in contributing to the loss, they are very adept at denying or deflecting blame, and they are often protected by the hospital or their medical association.

Despite these difficulties, there were some parents in this study who sought to reclaim their understanding of the circumstances around the death by resolving issues of real or perceived medical responsibility for their losses. One couple's child died while the woman was being prepared for a caesarean section; rather than wheeling her into the operating room as an emergency case, the obstetrician on call insisted on first performing a prebooked caesarean with his own patient. Although a subsequent autopsy showed that her son would almost certainly not have been saved by performing emergency surgery, this woman and her husband have still proceeded to make a case against this doctor with the Alberta College of Physicians. She explains:

He basically said, "I'll do her caesarean, but I'm doing my other lady first"—who was a booked caesarean. And so we had all this anger toward him, and it's being resolved now because we have seen lawyers. We can't proceed legally, we can't collect enough to make it worthwhile. But we wrote a letter to the College of Physicians and lodged a complaint against him, and they told me they are proceeding. So at least there will be something on the record that we have done something. So that at least in the future he can't do this to someone else. Whether my baby would have lived or not is not the issue because the doctor did not know that at the time. So I just think he acted shabbily.

For this couple, challenging a medical practitioner who they feel failed them has become a way to resolve their anger, redress some of the helplessness they suffered, and build on their own sense that something good might come out of their baby's death.

Parents who did make gestures of this nature also spoke of how uncharacteristic these actions were to them. Prior to the loss, they had never experienced anything that compelled them to take such actions. Pursuing the issue became not only a way to make a claim for their own loss, but to seize the opportunity to salvage some good for others from their experience.

Perhaps as complaints like this mount, physicians will begin to understand that a simple "these things happen" is no longer sufficient in addressing parental concerns. Perhaps autopsies on stillborn babies and late-term miscarriages might begin to be routinely performed in order to satisfy the unanswered questions parents are left asking, and perhaps physicians will be forced to understand that they can no longer treat perinatal loss in an off-hand fashion. One can hope.

REACT TO THE SEPARATION

Reacting to the separation occurs in three ways: mourners must first experience the pain, they must identify and mourn secondary losses, and then they must give some expression to the pain (Rando, 1993, p. 47).

Experience the pain

Rando (1993, p. 47) tells us that if the loss is to be accommodated the mourner must experience the pain of separation. In perinatal death, women are encouraged to numb themselves with drugs before, during and after delivery. They are given medication to stop their pain during delivery, to dry up their breast-milk in the days that follow it, and to ease their depression in the long term. Both parents receive social cues that encourage them to minimize the expression of their pain and to move quickly through their grief. Nonetheless, parents do feel pain, even when they really do not want to. Perhaps there are parents who feel nothing, who carry on and shoulder the load; however, because of the nature of this study, none of those parents volunteered to share their stories.

There were men and women who spoke of feeling little immediately after their loss, instead following the advice of seemingly wiser souls that the best medicine would be to get on with life and put this sad chapter behind them. For these people, regardless of their desire to feel little and grieve less, those feelings did eventually demand to be experienced. Feelings of pain often came up and were processed in unique and unexpected ways. One woman describes how she finally confronted her feelings:

> I signed up for this Art Therapy course, and we had to do an assessment of five pieces of work that belonged to a client or that we had done ourselves, and the theme had to be the family. This was over a year after the baby died. So I had decided to do my own work, and I went down to my studio and started drawing, and the first picture I did was a picture of a foetus, and then one of myself, pregnant and just so sad, and then of my husband—and he was literally castrated, and his hands were empty—and, like, it was just all laid out there for me to see—I just couldn't avoid it any longer, and then I called my husband down and said, "We have to talk."

This woman, expecting to complete her project as part of a course designed to help others, was quite unprepared for the feelings that overwhelmed her. She used this window of pain to reexamine the feelings both she and her husband had preferred to ignore, entering into both individual and joint therapy with her husband to work through their feelings.

Identify and mourn secondary losses

It is not always easy to identify the secondary losses attached to the death of a baby. When a living relationship with another has ended, the lack of companionship or support is eventually quite apparent. In the death of an infant, those secondary losses are less obvious and often relate to lost role potential or lost hopes, dreams or expectations. Many parents in this study entered into therapy at some point in their bereavement, often as secondary losses came up and needed to be addressed. Therapeutic involvement occurred in two ways: parents either sought to deal directly with their child's loss, or they came with other issues at the forefront and found that their grief became an unexpected focus. Either way, secondary losses came to be understood as a necessary focus of their grieving. One woman describes how her therapy, which she entered to help her deal with the death of her son, led her to review other aspects of herself:

> I mean, we dealt with the pregnancy thing quite well within the first few months and then after that it was other "stuff," you know, that had resurfaced by this loss. Feelings of inadequacy, feelings of rejection, feelings of humiliation, feelings of not being good enough, good enough for who? Good enough for the grandfather that upped and offed? Well, he wasn't good enough for me. So, yeah, it did bring out a lot of other issues.

This woman had wished very much to provide a grandson to her father-in-law to cement her position within the family. Her referral to him as the man who "upped and offed" is a result of his leaving town immediately after the baby's death and his refusing to attend the funeral. Only in therapy did she see that her feelings of inadequacy had as much to do with her feelings about this man as they did with her "failure" to give birth. Although grief for her dead child was the catalyst for entering therapy, her major task was to understand the ripple effect of his death on her self-esteem and her family relationships.

Conversely, many parents undertook therapy for other reasons and only came to understand while in therapy that the loss of their child was a primary loss. Because of the ambiguous nature of a preterm infant's death, it can happen that parents only come to see their perinatal grief as legitimate when it comes to light during therapy for more "legitimate" losses. One woman describes such a situation:

> I just had so much grief going on in my life at that time. I was working through some family-of-origin stuff and having a midlife crisis about what I was going to do with my life and trying to raise a kid and worrying that my marriage was falling apart. All this shit was going on. And it never really occurred to me that losing a baby might be part of that pain. And one day, my therapist pushed me to talk about the death directly, and I couldn't believe how much feeling welled up in me. And then I couldn't stop talking about her (laughs).

Whether parents come into a helping relationship with a primary agenda of dealing with their grief, or whether they enter therapy for other reasons and come to grief-work indirectly, it is clear that working through loss means confronting and understanding both primary and secondary issues.

The understanding that primary and secondary losses are interdependent is something that has come about in part due to the lobbying and (to use an old-fashioned word) consciousness-raising that has been done by perinatal loss support groups. These groups have educated hospitals, social workers, bereavement counselors, and funeral workers in order to raise the awareness of perinatal loss as a legitimate grief issue and to provide insight into the broad range of personal issues that are affected by the death of an infant. This education has taken the form of support groups, self-published litera-ture, educational presentations to professionals, and the distribution of information to bereaved parents. The net result is that both grief workers and newly bereaved parents are increasingly more prepared to understand that when a baby dies the loss is profound and the effects are far-reaching.

Give expression to the loss

According to Rando (1993), "unacknowledged and unexpressed emotion is a major source of pathology...mourners [must] overcome social, cultural, ethnic, or religious resistances" to the expression of grief (p. 47). Parents in this study faced tremendous social and cultural resistance to the expression of their grief and yet often managed to find deeply personal and powerful ways to give expression to their sorrow.

Traditionally, parents have not always been encouraged to have a funer-al for their child, particularly when the pregnancy has not gone to full-term. This, too, is beginning to change in reaction to increased awareness on the part of hospitals, social workers and clergy that ritual is as necessary to heal the wounds of perinatal loss as it is for any loss. Many parents in my sam-ple opted to have some sort of commemorative ritual, ranging from a tradi-tional funeral involving the entire community to a small memorial service in the hospital chapel attended by a select few. In these rituals, parents were very concerned to incorporate symbolic acts of parenting into the funeral rituals. Babies were dressed in pretty little outfits, given toys and stuffed animals to "keep them company" and given blankets to keep them warm. Again, the parents used the occasion as an opportunity to provide care for their babies. One couple bought a lovely blanket to wrap their baby girl in, cutting it in half: half was buried with her, and the other half remains with them as a keepsake.

Gestures of tenderness were often made in the seemingly somber, dark world of the funeral home. A couple of parents in this study were insistent that their children be laid in a bassinet rather than a coffin for their funer-als. I saw photos of one set of female twins, laid in frilly, lace-lined, pink bassinets that had been lovingly hand-decorated by the parents. The trappings of these little girls' burial were not typical of funerary paraphernalia—no marble, mahogany or brass. Rather, the parents had made their girls' last "home" look much like a baby's room, all sweetness and light.

In the interviews, parents provided loving and detailed descriptions of what they did for their children and why they chose to include this toy to "keep company" with their child or that particular outfit "so she would look pretty." These gestures are highly symbolic—they represent all the love and care that parents will ever have the opportunity to provide directly to their children.

It is important to note that the parents who made these gestures often were able to do so only after fighting strenuously with physicians, family members and funeral directors. Several women described how they were discouraged from seeing or handling their babies in funeral homes, and one woman's mother sought actively to keep her from even attending the funeral. The fight that these people undertook to create their own rituals was something they often described as being as much a surprise to them as to those they struggled against. One woman explains:

> I said to my husband, "I want to go back before the cremation and see her again." Because even at that point there were things that I needed that physical body there for, in order to express things that had changed from, you know, 3 days before. I had 20 years to cram into that. And the funeral director had a lot of difficulty with that. And I just wouldn't back down, which is just not like me.

This woman acknowledges that her need to carve out territory and to defend her decisions has changed her irrevocably. The same woman explains how she has changed:

> It just changed my life. I mean, that's not who I am, who I was. I was very quiet. I had nothing to say—I never did have anything to say, and it wasn't because I was stupid or anything. Now I have lots to say. I mean, I just have a different insight now. I just know what's really important enough to stand up for.

This woman's experience of fighting for something she believed in, and winning, has given her a new strength and wisdom.

Parents who did not have the opportunity to provide direct gestures of care found ways to act out their care indirectly. Parents spoke of planting a tree or making a donation in the dead child's name years later. One woman spoke of how sorry she had been that she did not name a daughter who had died 6 years earlier. Lately, she has begun to use the name that she and her husband had chosen, in effect naming her child posthumously. She explains:

> No, we did not really do anything at the time. We did not even think of it because there was no birth certificate or anything. And I've felt bad about that. But lately I've begun talking about her to my husband again because I do not think we dealt with it enough then. I use her name—I even did that with my mother on her last visit out here. And she really reacted differently. Like, if my baby had a name, then she was real after all.

Giving her child a name, even 6 years later, has provided a way for her and her family members to legitimate and acknowledge the loss. Further, by giving her child a name, she has been able to let go of the regrets she felt for not performing the gesture at the time of the baby's death. In essence, she has coopted the traditional norm of naming a living child, using it to give her dead child legitimacy.

Another way that parents find to give expression to their feelings is through reading and, particularly, writing. A number of women described keeping a journal following their children's deaths and how doing so was a new activity for them. I also received poetry from several people. For these writers, the purpose of the writing is not necessarily to publish but to give voice to feelings that otherwise will not be expressed in any other way.

Parents also used their interviews with me as a forum for expressing their feelings of loss. Almost without exception, parents arrived at interviews carrying bundles that represented their dead children. For some parents, the bundles consisted of little that was personally related to the dead child. Here, a woman describes for me what is contained in the envelope she has brought to the interview with her:

> The social worker gave me this book—it's called "Losing a Baby." Have you seen this booklet? It was quite helpful. So I read that quite a bit, and quite a few people from back home wrote lovely letters. And I got these cards, which I found very, very helpful. I just keep them at my bedside in my drawer (laughs). This [the book], and the cards, then a couple of letters that people had written.

For this woman, the record of other peoples' acknowledgments acts as an affirmation that she has suffered a loss, while the existence of a book on the topic confirms that such a loss is real enough to merit publication. Bringing these items to an interview, and sharing them with me, is a symbolic way of bearing witness.

The very act of giving an interview on the subject of perinatal loss, of representing these mementoes to another person (myself), of adding to a public study on the topic, of providing a photocopy of one's diary or poems, these are all ways of giving expression to the loss. Many people admitted that a primary motive for participating in the study was to take the opportunity to express their grief and be heard. As the following woman said at the end of her interview:

> No, nothing more to add. I think I've given you pretty well the full story. And I do find that this is what I need, like I find I seem to need that cleansing. I need to explain to somebody that will listen for a change, every once in a while.

As this woman states, finding someone to listen is not always that easy, and parents are willing to grab whatever ear presents itself to express their grief.

The various "ears" that parents will appropriate for the expression of their grief include support groups and individual therapists. As I stated in an earlier chapter, bereaved parents would definitely prefer that their audience be a sympathetic circle of intimates; however, in the all-too-likely event that family and friends fail them, parents who are resourceful and who adopt a postmodern willingness to go beyond traditional sources will find appropriate surrogates to fill the gap.

RECOLLECT AND REEXPERIENCE THE DECEASED AND THE RELATIONSHIP WITH THE DECEASED

When Rando (1993) discusses this process of grieving, she separates it into two aspects: first, mourners must review their relationship with the deceased in order to understand what that relationship meant to them and thus what its loss means; and second, mourners must reexperience and then let go of the feelings that were a part of their relationship with the deceased (p. 48).

Review and remember realistically

It is very difficult for parents to review and remember the lives of their children. There is so little to recall besides dreams and hopes. Although "remembering" a relationship that has not yet occurred seems impossible, parents were able to do this symbolically. They consistently described how they collected mementoes or made particular decisions as to funeral practices or made symbolic gestures shortly after the losses, speaking of these acts as ways of "creating memories." Special toys were purchased; sometimes they were included in the coffin, and in other instances, they were brought home and set up in special places. One woman describes the way that all members of her family created a web of memories around her stillborn daughter:

> I made a little outfit for her, for her to be cremated in. And my husband sewed—my husband who's never sewed anything before in his life—sewed a little teddy bear for her—it was just a little rabbit sewn together and a little face embroidered on it, and that rabbit took on this kind of grimace, so my husband said, "This little bunny will protect her no matter where she is." And my children went to the mall and got beads, and each one made her a little bracelet. And we wanted to give her this gift before she was cremated.

By creating rituals, and by involving the entire family in that creation, this woman has also created a series of memories that are meaningful for all the members of her family. She has little difficulty discussing her dead child with her living children and with her husband because they *know* the little girl: they all said hello, they all said goodbye, and they all share some very real memories that they themselves created around the dead child.

This type of memory, seemingly, is never too late to create. One woman, despite having a traditional funeral for a dead child several years ago, has still found little acknowledgement within her community because she is a Mormon. Mormons believe that family members all live in heaven, coming to earth only for a short period and returning to the "real" family once their earthly work is done. Thus, for a Mormon to feel inconsolable grief over a death is not acceptable and can be interpreted by fellow Mormons as a lack of faith.

In order to get around her community's inability to acknowledge her pain, this woman has had to be extremely creative in creating memories that indirectly include her dead child in the community. Since direct expressions of grief are unacceptable, she has begun collecting angel figurines and paraphernalia, and the collection has been contributed to by many members of her family and community. For her, the angels are symbolic of her baby and act as a "shrine" for her dead child. For the members of her family and community, this symbolism remains unacknowledged. Thus, public discussion of the angels is not couched in terms of the baby; instead, they focus on "the angel that I gave you last year" or "the angel I brought back from our last trip. " In this way, she is able to create memories that her dead child is symbolically a part of the community while at the same time maintaining appropriate community standards of grieving.

Many parents describe having special Christmas tree ornaments for their dead children so that those children can be with them symbolically at that special family time. The names of dead children are often included in family trees, on roll calls at family reunions, and in family photo albums. This inclusion has two implications: first, parents are creating memories that enable them to make their child more real; and second, the inclusion makes the loss more real to significant others, increasing the chance of validation by family and friends.

Revive and reexperience the feelings

Rando (1993) notes that mourners must, over time, untie all of the bonds that hold them to the lost one. All of the hopes, wishes and fantasies about that person and the relationship must be assessed and reversed. According to Rando (1993), when this process is done successfully, the ties that bind "are modified to reflect the change that the loved one is now dead...and a new relationship ultimately must be developed because the old one is unworkable" (p. 50).

It is difficult for a parent to create a new relationship when the old one has not been fully developed. Parenting is simply not comprehensible in advance; rather, it is a role that is accomplished piecemeal—the stages of a child's development are often accompanied by major changes in the parent's life, in the relationship between parent and child, and in the feelings that exist between parent and child. Parents who suffer perinatal loss must come to terms with letting go of the expected bonds of parenting on a piecemeal basis as well by confronting each stage of what could have been and releasing that part of the wished-for relationship. Thus, new aspects of loss are often triggered by the baptism of a friend's baby or the first family Christmas after the baby's death or a subsequent pregnancy.

Parental responses to triggering events, which Rando calls STUGS, are pivotal in working through grief on an ongoing basis. There were a number of parents in my study who dealt well with these STUGS. One woman describes how she sought, and got, what she needed from her mother on one such occasion:

> The day, the due date, I was kinda surprised that she didn't know why I was calling. But I phoned and I was just so upset, and I was dressed and ready for work. I'd been up for hours trying to get ready for work. And I phoned her and I was just crying, and I said, "Mom, today's the

due date," and she said did not know if it was, and I said, "I'm not doing well." And she just cried with me.

Although at first her need for support was not clearly understood or acknowledged, she was able to insist on getting some sympathy. Her mother came through and, what is more, learned that the due date is an important one to recall—she has not forgotten it since.

RELINQUISH OLD ATTACHMENTS TO THE DECEASED AND THE OLD ASSUMPTIVE WORLD

Rando (1993) describes one's assumptive world as "an organized schema containing everything a person assumes to be true about the world and the self on the basis of previous experience" (p. 50). The attachments that exist for parents mourning a child lost through perinatal death are based on assumptions about parenting that are often unrealistic. Parents often assume they are totally responsible for their children's care and that they are subsequently responsible for any harm that befalls their children. As a result, the central emotion that parents of a too-soon dead child must deal with is guilt.

There were a number of parents in this study who found appropriate ways to deal with and release that guilt. One woman surprised me when I asked her whether she had ever experienced any feelings of guilt:

I've read that a lot of women feel guilt. And although I guess I did consider it, that did not last long because I knew it wasn't my fault. I am faith-filled, and I think when I spoke to the priest 2 weeks after it was really helpful. I had often heard people say "it must be for a reason" and that had never made any sense to me. But the priest put it differently. He said, "No, there's not necessarily a reason, but perhaps we can find some *meaning* from these things."

For this woman, her baby's death has become the impetus for seeking spiritual meaning in her life, and it has led her to reevaluate what she counts as important.

Only one other woman in the study was clear that she had no feelings of guilt. In her case, the medical advice she was given worked to absolve her of responsibility. The advice this woman received went well beyond her physician merely shrugging her shoulders and saying "these things just happen":

What I was told when I went to the hospital and when the doctor came to see me was that it was nothing that I did. She said it was first thing that I had to know. That I did nothing, and that I had to believe that. And I think that helped me. Because they told me, and I accepted that and haven't ever second-guessed it.

Perhaps the clarity with which the message was delivered made her able to fully accept that she really had no part in causing the death. Perhaps another reason this woman was able to let any feelings of responsibility and guilt go was because she ultimately did hold someone else responsible. This woman is the same woman described above who has lodged a formal complaint against the obstetrician who delayed her Caesarean section in order to serve his own patient. Whether her lack of guilt stems from her ability to lay blame elsewhere or, as she believes, from being clearly and repeatedly advised by those in authority *not* to blame herself, it would seem that there is no harm in physicians telling parents clearly and repeatedly that self-blame is simply not appropriate.

Besides being clearly absolved of guilt by authorities, I believe the symbolic acts of parenting exemplified by putting a blanket in with the baby in the coffin, dressing and bathing the baby, or providing special little toys for the child are crucial in reducing feelings of guilt. In a way, anticipated roles can be let go more readily because they have been fulfilled through these gestures. By acting out the protective and caring parts of the role, parents can gain a glimmer of understanding of what becoming a parent meant to them; they can experience the positive, nurturing aspects of parenting and can let go of feelings of inadequacy and remorse.

READJUST, MOVE ADAPTIVELY INTO THE NEW WORLD WITHOUT FORGETTING THE OLD

According to Rando (1993), before an individual can let go of their past ties with the deceased and move into a new relationship with them, and a new way of being, they must deal with how the loss assailed their assumptions, both global (about themselves, life, and the world in general) and specific (their specific hopes and expectations for interaction with the deceased) (pp. 51–53).

Revise the assumptive world

Parents deal with their specific assumptions about their relationship with the hoped-for child at the same time as they are "creating memories." Symbolically, many of the same hopes and expectations they held before the baby died were acted out and transformed in their inclusion of their children in family events, in family holidays, and in family commemorations. In a sense, they continue to parent, although the parenting is performed in a highly symbolic fashion. In doing this, it becomes possible for parents to maintain their assumptions about what kind of parents they would have been or how sweet and loving their relationship with their children would have been had they lived. Parents do not revise their assumptions about parenting when they act out the role symbolically; rather, they maintain their assumptions by these acts.

Parents in this study often did revise their global assumptions, primarily by reevaluating their sense of self. Parents who thought themselves to be resilient and strong had to work through an understanding of themselves that contradicted those beliefs, while parents who thought that they could accomplish whatever they set their minds to had to deal with the reality of failure in their lives.

Some parents were highly creative in dealing with failure by reframing their grief as a triumph. A number of them described how "having gone through this, I know that I can just about handle anything. I mean, I know that I am strong and that nothing much can defeat me." These parents speak of themselves as being tougher than they thought they ever could have been and couched this new aspect of themselves in terms of growth and self-knowledge rather than as a mere response to failure:

> I think I lost some naivete during the whole process, which maybe isn't a bad thing. I think, up until that point if I wanted something I seemed to be able to get it, if I worked hard enough. And I think it was the first big obstacle that I came up against that I could do on my own. That, for example, in terms of dealing with the medical community, you do not just give up after they shut you down. I often think we've gained some wisdom through this and some perseverance.

Other parents had to revise their concepts of themselves as competent and resilient people who were in charge of their lives. One woman explains how her self-concept as a woman in control came to be altered:

> There were just days where I'd forget where I was going. I'd actually got to the point where I was fearful of driving. So the only thing that I would do is go get my daughter and that was it. I wouldn't drive alone. I was scared because I thought I was gonna lose it. I mean, even to the point of forgetting to pick my daughter up from school, and they'd call, and I'd just be amazed. I'd think, "How could I be a mother—how

could I give such poor care?" For a while I was worried whether I could look after my children.

This woman's sense of competence, of being collected and capable was confronted by the reality of being so preoccupied and in pain that she could barely handle her most basic responsibilities. This struck at the core of her self-esteem. Nonetheless, she came to understand that this experience with vulnerability had its own benefits:

> When I think about what I used to be like—I was so unforgiving. I never understood people who did not just bounce back from things because I was very much that way. It's turned my life upside down. Just realizing what people go through is number one, and secondly, just how life can hurt your heart so bad.

Like other resilient parents in this study, she has interpreted the blow dealt to her self-knowledge as growth. Her baby died for something, if only to teach her humility.

Yet another global assumption that mourners were forced to revise was the belief that the world is a safe and predictable place and that experts are competent and reliable. Experts in this case include medical practitioners, funeral directors, and clergy. A number of parents found hitherto unknown resourcefulness in challenging the advice of medical authorities and funeral directors.

Not only have these parents learned to question experts and authorities in medical or service industries, but they have also learned that a lot of "folk wisdom" and "common knowledge" about how they should handle their loss is not reliable—they have learned to question society's feeling rules and have become willing to carve out their own ways of seeing and feeling things:

> One of the good things that came out of [baby's] death was I was getting a lot of support, like in terms of nursing staff and counselors. It made me recognize that this was something that I was allowed to do, and if my mother treated me like I was not allowed to do it, she was wrong. Like she did not have a right to treat me like this because I had a right to feel the way I did.

Because of the depth of the feelings her child's death raised, this woman came to understand that her lived feelings held authority over what she was told she should feel, both in direct relation to her grief and in other areas of her life as well.

Develop a new relationship with the deceased

Rando (1993) explains that developing a healthy new relationship with the deceased does not mean "putting the past behind" or breaking all connections to the loved one; rather, it means developing an "appropriate" connection in a revised relationship with the deceased. Appropriate to Rando (1993) means that the mourner must "truly recognize that the person is dead, and must continue to move forward adaptively into a new life" (p. 55).

Parents in this study were very creative in establishing a new relationship with their dead children. Raising a child usually means hopes for the future and expectations of a lifelong and loving relationship. For a number of parents, having a child die did not mean the end to that possibility; rather, it simply meant that their relationship with the dead child would have to wait until after their own death. Many parents, including those who categorized themselves as having no strong religious ties, were adamant that they would see their children again after death. For parents who were religious, the child was clearly existing in a better spiritual place, waiting to resume the relationship. One woman describes her beliefs about her son:

> I do not know all the theology, I just know that in my heart that [baby] is in Heaven. Like, 2 or 3 days after he was born—I do not want to say it was a vision, but it was like an image that I had of him, of [the baby]. I saw him as a 2-year-old with blonde, curly hair, holding Jesus' hand. The image of Jesus that I had was of a tall man, dark hair, with long, flowing light robes. They were walking along, and Jesus was walking with his eyes straight ahead, and [baby] was holding his hand and looking backwards (laughs)—children often do—you know, they're looking behind them. It was at that point that I had a real comfort that he was in a better place and that he was going to be taken care of.

For this woman, as for many others I spoke with, the child they lost has simply moved to a safer, kinder place, perhaps a place that is more deserving of an innocent and perfect child than the world that child left behind.

Parents who feel this way have no doubt that they will someday be reunited with their children. The relationship that they expect to have with their children is changed—it will not be a parent-child relationship as they would have expected it to be on earth, but they remain certain that their child will remain a child until they are reunited in the afterlife. Simultaneously, the baby in heaven is often seen as a guardian angel who watches over parents while waiting for parents to arrive in heaven and pick up the relationship where it left off. Again, this is a highly creative reworking of parenting practices and of popular culture. The angel theme is currently very common in books and in popular visual arts, but parents in this case have created a personal relationship with an angel, taking the popular form one step further. Likewise, they have reformed cultural ideals of parenting into something that transcends life, death and time—a number of parents referred to a belief that although their other children would grow up and away the dead baby would "always be a baby to me."

There were a number of parents who did not comfort themselves with a vision of some future reunion. For them, letting go of the relationship they expected to have with their baby did not involve delaying the hopes and dreams of parenting until some later date; rather, it meant changing the direction of those hopes and dreams in the here and now. These were parents who sought to find some way of taking the love and selflessness they had intended to employ as parents and divert it to a social or moral good. A number of parents spoke about how their experiences had taught them to value all life more. Almost all spoke of being better lovers, friends, and parents because of this deeper understanding of life's preciousness. One woman describes how her family relationships have changed since her loss:

> Having her made my other children more valuable. It made my tie with my husband more valuable. It made things a lot more clear to me. When I think what my life was like, I was playing house. You know, life was a set of behaviors that I went through, and I acted out this role as a mother. And my life now is different in the fact that I recognize now what's important. Like, spiritually I feel good.

The spiritual well-being this woman describes comes from a mature understanding of what counts and a willingness to fully honor others in her life in ways that her loss helped her to see.

Adopt new ways of being in the world

Rando (1993, p. 59) states that for mourners to become healthy they cannot continue to behave in ways they did when the loved ones were alive, and the way to do this is to find ways to fulfill the needs the deceased had previously filled, either through new loved ones or through a new focus that will fill that old need. As with many other elements of Rando's typology, a direct application to perinatal mourners is problematic precisely because there never has been a relationship or way of being that entailed the baby when he/she was alive. Thus, parents in this study did not really work out new ways of being that reflected the loss of the actual child; rather, they adopted new ways of being that reflected a changed relationship to themselves and their beliefs about themselves.

The experience of loss left some parents unwilling to accept superficial or unsatisfying relationships. A number of people reported experiencing changes in both old and new relationships. As one woman said,

> I find distance between myself and some of my old friends. The people that I hang out with now have generally experienced the same kind of loss. It's just that they understand where I'm at...and there is a woman I've met who also lost a baby and who would not be good friends under other circumstances, but we've become very good friends, and she will be my friend now, for probably the rest of my life.

The relationship these two women have created through their common understanding is simply one example of many that parents described in this study. These relationships are deeper and more honest than what parents had typically known. The richness of those relationships is only possible because of the wisdom gained through loss.

Another woman described how she and her husband, who were new to Calgary and therefore quite isolated, were taken under the wings of another couple and what that relationship has meant to both her and her husband:

> There was one couple that we kind of knew here in Calgary, just acquaintances really, and they were great. They took us to Windermere for a weekend to—they rented a cabin there. And she was having infertility problems at the time, but she did not tell me that. But she mothered me, and I needed that. And we're still incredibly good friends, and they're the godparents of my son.

Although the woman in the other couple had not suffered a pregnancy loss, there are parallels between infertility and pregnancy loss, so the relationship these couples were able to develop was based on a common understanding of loss.

Parents not only gave more in their intimate relationships after losing a child, but they described giving more to the general community and to unknown others. Several women discussed reaching out to barely known acquaintances when they heard those people had suffered losses. They called, dropped by to visit, or sent notes of condolence and understanding. They were also convinced that they would never have made a gesture like that before their own loss.

Other parents spoke of a desire to contribute to their world, to give from the well of their new understanding. They now know that life is fleeting and that opportunities for positive work must be seized as they occur. Thus, the woman who became a minister described caring for her parishioners as a way of expressing the love that she would have given to her child. She has turned his death into an act of sacrifice, an event that forced her to express her best self in public acts rather than through private gestures of mothering. A number of women made these observations, saying they never would have gone to school, gone into nursing, become a minister, been as good a physician, or held the same high values if they had not lost a child.

Participants spoke of gaining a new sense of perspective. One woman told me "it changes you—when you get stuck behind a slow driver on the highway—I mean, you just learn what's important." Another woman spoke of how her priorities had changed regarding subsequent babies: the 3 a.m. feed for her became a gift rather than a chore.

Form a new identity

Rando (1993, p. 59) says that the person who has worked through the internal and social changes described above will, of course, have developed a new identity and that accepting one's new self-knowledge is a necessary step in the grieving process. Almost all of the parents I spoke with acknowledged that their experiences had left them changed. Parents were creative in their interpretation of those changes; in a sense, they claimed to have rebirthed themselves as a by-product of the "failed" births of their children. One woman's description is particularly well-stated:

> When my daughter died, it felt like I had this blanket thrown over my head, and everything I saw and everything that I did had been colored by that light shining through the blanket. Everything looked so much different than it ever did before. I still live under that light for the rest of my life. Before, I was just filling in time, really. But now I say, "Well, why? Like what is the point?" And I think that is part of that spiritual change. I think you live a lot more—you focus more on what your life is like. And I think that's good.

This woman's comments reflect a common experience: that the change and the new spirituality have been difficult and came unsought. Yet, from that different light, from the ashes of loss, there is something profoundly positive to be reclaimed. Life is now seen as richer, sweeter, and never to be taken for granted again. In this sense, the death, and the subsequent pain in mourning it, becomes a way to claim a second chance, to grow and become wiser, and ultimately to feel gratitude for the new wisdom that death has made possible.

REINVEST

In her discussion, Rando (1993) refers to new investments in "other people, objects, roles, hopes, beliefs, causes and ideals" as ways for mourners to redirect the emotional energy that was part of their relationship to the deceased in ways that are new and growth-oriented. In my sample, parents who were highly creative used the new wisdom and insight they gained through their loss to move on to different ways of living their lives. For some parents, that meant taking on new pregnancies or investing their energies in reformulated relationships as parents, partners or community members. For others, it meant going into new areas of work with a focus on social justice or healing. For yet others, it meant revising the way they approached their old work. One woman, a physician, describes how her approach has been altered:

I have done it myself: gone off duty and had hand-over and said, "Well, I've seen four abortions in the Gyne room and a heart in Room 6 and a G.I. bleed in Room 4." As though they weren't people, just diagnoses. And I would *never* do that now. It's changed my practice. It's made it easier for the patients because I really feel what they're going through, and they know, and I *tell* them. I find myself putting my arms around the person and crying with them. And it's no longer an issue as a physician, you know, if the tears come because I've learned we have to allow ourselves to feel.

This woman, like many others who have negotiated the tortuous path of grief, has found a way to integrate her new perspective into a new and better self.

Most, but not all, parents in my study had reached some place of acceptance in their grief. Bereaved parents who are willing to understand their loss as an opportunity and who are able to find creative and personally meaningful ways to resolve the complicating factors in perinatal mourning are able to come through their experiences not only changed, but enlarged. Parents who interpret their loss as an opportunity to grow and learn are able to let their children go and understand that despite the brief tenure of their lives their children have been able to profoundly affect the world. Their lives meant something. Honoring and giving expression to that meaning becomes reason enough for these parents to carry on.

CONCLUSION

There was not one parent in this study who seemed to have been able to negotiate the course of grief without finding some particular aspect quite painful or difficult to resolve. The woman who so beatifically reported her vision of her child with Jesus was the same woman whose husband needed the experience of combat in Yugoslavia before he and she could find a common ground for their feelings. The woman who spoke about how she no longer merely plays house since her loss but has come to value her family and her spirituality in a new way is the same woman who described going to her physician's house at night with the intent of killing her, and she is also the woman who discussed her own body size so disparagingly. The man who steadfastly blamed his wife's body for their loss was the same man who so creatively found a way to save his wife from coming out of the hospital with empty arms by buying her a stuffed animal. Thus, attempting to draw conclusions about what kind of person can negotiate perinatal grief best or comparing different subsets of this sample to conclude which factors result in relatively "uncomplicated" mourning would simply not capture the complexity of these parents' lives.

Many parents whose social networks should have provided them with adequate resources to negotiate their feelings found themselves suffering many years later. Others, who were isolated and alone, managed to find solace in unanticipated quarters. Sometimes, religion helped people to find meaning; for others, such as the Mormon woman who came from a close-knit religious community, religion became a problem in and of itself. Gestational age and length of time since the loss also bore little effect on how much pain parents suffered. It is not that simple.

However, one man and one woman in this sample did strike me as having done relatively little grief processing compared to the other participants. These parents, whose losses were quite old, remained distraught throughout their interviews, often had difficulty dealing with the emotional aspects of their loss, and were less able to explore all the areas of discussion that the other participants so willingly took on with me. Perhaps a clue as to why some parents get trapped can be found in what the man had to say when I asked him to discuss any "good" that might have come from his experiences:

Nothing really. I'd be interested to hear the comments you get back on that question—I bet there isn't anything! No, I wouldn't say that there was any.

For this man, there was no growth, there was no meaning, there was only pain. This same man, when asked why he chose to participate in this study, replied that he had really understood this to be a study on prevalence and causes of miscarriages, although I had been very clear in telling him the purpose of the interview. Unlike the other parents in this study, he could not see participating in research as a way to help others or learn more about himself through shared knowledge. Parents like this, whose understanding of their children's deaths is simply that this a bad thing that happened, seem to pay an extremely high price for that belief. Several years later, they are still struggling to make sense of their experiences.

The findings in this study can only be considered as particular to the individuals who participated in it. The sample size and characteristics mean that my analysis of perinatal loss cannot be generalized to "the way people experience the death of a baby." Rather, this analysis represents how some parents experienced their children's deaths and how I have understood their stories. I believe the analysis does provide insight into many of the "whys" and "hows" of perinatal grief.

Comparisons between different cultural or religious contexts should be explored in order to understand how the devastating effects of perinatal loss can be best mediated. Studies that examine the role of different gender-related belief systems (pronatalist versus childless-by-choice, traditionalist versus feminist, careerist versus homemaker) would be helpful in providing evidence to refute or support the "common wisdom" of the day that tells us that not wanting a child or having a job or other children or valuing one's womanhood over one's motherhood can lessen the pain of losing a baby. Further studies should also aim to expand our understanding of disenfranchised grief in perinatal loss to people beyond the parental dyad. In my literature review, I found no studies that directly examined siblings' feelings of loss; as in my own study, the question of sibling grief is typically subsumed as part of research with parents.

In the course of my research, I received a poem, written by the paternal uncle of a stillborn girl. It offers eloquent testimony to the shattered hopes and dreams this young man had to deal with when he lost his little niece. I must confess that even as someone who has first-hand experience of others not recognizing my loss as legitimate I myself never really considered what such a loss might mean to grandparents, aunts and uncles, or potential godparents. Future research should explore the experiences of these disenfranchised mourners.

Finally, the seemingly linear framework proposed by using Rando's typology of complicating factors and her six "R" processes should not be understood as a representation of "the way perinatal grief unfolds." Rather, the discussion I have opened up using her framework should be understood as just that—a framework. I prefer to think of each of Rando's factors and processes as questions rather than answers. There are undoubtedly additional questions to ask about the grieving process, and I hope this study will provide a springboard for them. Very little has been written that extensively dissects the social, psychological and physiological interplays in perinatal grief, so this research represents a contribution to our understanding of disenfranchised grief, complicated mourning, and postmodern creativity in response to the nonsocial deaths of pre- or at-term infants. Yet my study represents only a beginning of that understanding.

Chapter 7
Research as Therapeutic Process:
For Participants and Researcher Alike

Sociologists have examined almost every imaginable aspect of human life without wincing. Sociologists have joined motorcycles gangs, hung out with criminals, studied skinheads and acted as flies on the wall in insane asylums. Statistically, these populations are likely rarer than people who have suffered pregnancy loss; it is estimated that in the United States between 20% and 30% of all known pregnancies fail (Layne, 1990). I was surprised, then, to find just how little research had been done within sociology on this very common human phenomenon. Perhaps because the issue of perinatal loss is so intrinsically tied up with the sacred cows of both motherhood and death, it has been regarded as a topic best left unexplored. Or perhaps, as Reinharz (1988) speculates, social scientists are just as likely as other people to accept the common cultural belief that "miscarried fetuses are easily replaced by pregnancies brought to term" (p. 4). Reinharz (1988, p. 5) also speculates that feminists have skirted the issue because of its ambiguous relation to abortion and choice. For whatever reasons, there remains relatively little sociological research on the subject of perinatal loss.

Within my own Sociology department, I encountered resistance to researching perinatal loss. Concerns were raised that "there will be some marriages or marriage-like relationships which will fail as a result of this 'sore point' being raised again by you" (private correspondence, 1995). Those who were concerned went so far as to warn me off the project, saying, "If I were in your situation, the above may be sufficient to keep me from doing the research" (private correspondence, 1995). The departmental Ethics Committee suggested that a screening device be used to "preclude the involvement in this study of anyone for whom the miscarriage or stillbirth created significant problems in the relationship with the partner." As I suspected, and as was confirmed in the course of the research, such a caveat would virtually have excluded anyone who has suffered perinatal loss; relationship stress is seemingly an inevitable part of the postloss experience.

The final result of my struggle to gain departmental Ethics approval was a very lengthy consent form requiring considerable explanation and assurance. As well as the consent form, I handed out lists of counselors who are experts in the field of perinatal loss and pamphlets prepared by Caring Beyond, a local support group for bereaved parents. I often felt uncomfortable with this procedure because I worried it might set an anxious tone for the interviews rather than contribute to the relaxed, trusting atmosphere necessary for creating rapport. I wondered if the University's efforts to reassure people might actually cause participants to feel unnecessary angst.

My subjective sense was that the warnings about ill effects and the attempts to protect people from possible harm in participating in this research were overkill. My own feelings of isolation and inappropriateness while grieving had left me longing for someone with whom to talk. If I had an opportunity to know that others, too, had felt the same things, I believe it would have helped me. I suspected this was true for others. The silence that surrounds perinatal loss is a lonely one for those who suffer its consequences, and I hoped my research would contribute towards breaking the silence surrounding perinatal loss. I also felt that providing people with an opportunity to tell their stories might offer them the chance to know that their situation was not unique, bizarre, or unworthy of study. In short, I felt the very act of participating in research on perinatal loss would be therapeutic, empowering and healing.

I wanted to test these beliefs and assess the impact of research participation in this study. I must acknowledge that a second impetus for a follow-up survey was to determine whether or not I personally had made a difference for participants. The interviews that were granted to me were very intimate, highly emotional and profoundly thoughtful in content. In return, I felt personally touched, emotionally moved, and was led to reconsider aspects of my own grieving. I wanted to know whether these people were as changed by what they heard and said as I found myself to be. I also needed to be assured that I had not harmed people simply to satisfy my own need to know.

FOLLOW-UP SURVEY ON RESEARCH IMPACT

I was pleased to discover in my readings that I am not the only researcher who has faced such questions. Ebaugh (1988, pp. 213–224) discusses the therapeutic impact of information interviews. The therapeutic interview, traditionally performed in clinical settings, is based on a therapist-to-client interaction, with the goal of changing client cognitions and behaviors. The information interview is the domain of the social researcher, and its goal is to extract information of specific interest to the investigator. Ebaugh rightly states that often the two types overlap. Participants in information interviews can become highly emotional and may also be motivated to participate by a desire for therapeutic outcomes. In her own research, Ebaugh found a great deal of emotional outpouring from interview participants, and she began to wonder what impact the interview experience was having on her respondents. As a result of this finding, she developed a follow-up questionnaire to assess the impact of her research on respondents.

Following Ebaugh's general findings, I developed my own follow-up questionnaire. I was primarily interested in whether participation in the interview had changed any ideas or awareness for participants, whether participation had caused any changes in participants' relationships, and whether participation had been helpful or harmful. The questionnaire was composed primarily of open-ended questions, along with four fixed-response Likert scale questions. This survey was sent to all interview participants, with a covering letter that assured respondents' anonymity. The letter asked them to complete the questionnaire and invited them to add comments or questions.

It seems my concern for anonymity was not that important to my respondents. Several of the respondents included identifying statements or put their names and addresses on the envelopes containing their replies. Therefore, I have been able to accurately use feminine pronouns in my analysis because all the respondents quoted in this section were female.

Ten of the 25 participants responded, with no follow-up. The size of this subsample is obviously not large enough to make any claims to validity or generalizability, but again, this is an exploratory study, and I have analyzed the responses in that light.

Changed awareness or understanding

None of the respondents cited a search for knowledge on miscarriage as one of their goals in participating in the research. Nonetheless, when asked directly about new understanding that came from participation, it seems people did gain insight into their loss and its effects.

Two people said they had gained a new understanding of perinatal loss. One woman found that going over the story of her loss in such unusual detail really gave her a new perspective on how pivotal her babies had been in her life, saying, "I realize how very special the twins are more so now than before." For her, the opportunity of examining her story in one extensive piece provided her with a fuller perspective on the loss. The other woman said she was now aware that her experience is similar to and connected with the experiences of others, saying, "I learned that my reaction to loss, although maybe slightly different in some respects, is quite universal." For this woman, participation meant learning that she is not alone and that her experience is, in fact, quite normal. This woman's insight is a positive one, particularly in light of the commonly reported experience parents had of fearing that their grief was pathological.

One woman, through her participation, came to understand just how little support she was really getting within her community. She says,

> I felt angry when I realized how much I was dealing with before, during and after my loss. I do not get support from my husband or family at all.

She had been struggling alone and suppressing her feelings. Talking her whole situation through to a relatively impartial listener provided her with the opportunity to see her situation from a new perspective.

For some parents, the depth of the feelings they still held came as a surprise. They said things like, "I was surprised at how close to the surface the pain is even today," or "I was surprised at how emotional I felt when I spoke of the symbolism of my family ring" (how she commemorated her dead babies). Although this emotion came as a surprise, parents also expressed "how good it was to walk through those feelings again." As one woman states:

> It has been almost 2 years, and during the interview it seemed like yesterday. It choked me up, and I shed some tears, but I felt better after. I was surprised at myself. Claudia was also very understanding and sympathetic, and I never expected that. It was good for me to do this.

In a sense, the interview was an opportunity to review the events in their entirety, to reexperience some of the feelings, and to let them go. One of Rando's (1993) six "R" processes, "Recollect and Reexperience the Deceased and the Relationship," includes the subphases in which the mourner's work is to "Review and Remember" and to "Revive and Reexperience the

Feelings" (p. 44). Participating in this research provided some parents with the opportunity to do just that, and so it may have actually facilitated further grief resolution.

Changed relationships

In response to a direct question regarding effects of research participation on people's relationships, 6 of 10 people reported no effect at all, and four people reported positive outcomes from their participation. Two people reported that their marital relationship was affected; one woman spoke about a shift in her relationship with her son; and another spoke of how feeling a connection with the researcher had affected her.

A primary concern of the departmental Ethics Committee was that participation in this research would cause or contribute to marital breakdown for respondents. Three women spoke of how their involvement in the research related to their relationships with their partners. One woman said, "My husband was so pleased that I had been able to take part in this research—he knew I needed a better ear than his—and I appreciated his concern." This couple was able to use the catalyst of research involvement to express positive feelings of support for one another, even though they did not undertake direct discussion of grief issues. Another couple used the woman's involvement in the research as an opportunity to reopen discussion, saying, "We talked lots about the interview and shared our feelings about the twins." A third woman said that her marital relationship had not been affected but that she never gets any support from her husband about this issue. It seems that the research experience merely acted to highlight ongoing relationship patterns between partners. If the marriage typically included positive communication, the interview provided a forum for discussion, but if there was no support in the marriage, the interview pointed that up as well.

One woman wrote back with a beautiful account of how her relationship to her son had been affected by the interview:

I am closer with my 6-year-old son. You asked me if I had discussed my miscarriages with him. I had not, but your question encouraged me to bring it up. About 2–3 weeks later, he was very discouraged about going to school and was making shocking statements like, "I don't like being me," etc. Over breakfast I told him my story and explained to him how special and important he was to me. He had many questions. One of them was how old would the oldest child have been. I told him 8 years old and he assumed it would have been a brother.

At lunch he had more questions and really felt sad that he did not have an 8-year-old brother. After school the subject came up again. We sat on the sofa together, and he cried for about 20 minutes—it was the strongest mourning I have ever seen him demonstrate. The result was that he started to see his little sister as special and started to treat her a lot better. He also knows how special he is. Thanks, Claudia, for the question.

Using the postmodern creativity I described in the previous chapter, this wise woman was able to learn from her participation, and she used her new insight to bring her understanding of loss and its relation to her living children to a higher level.

A final changed relationship was expressed by one woman's comment that she "felt a connection with the interviewer...I knew I shared an experience with her that no one who has not experienced the same thing can fully understand." This woman and I, like others in the study, have maintained contact since the interview. Although we have not yet become friends, I can see the possibility of friendship. There have been rewards for both of us in doing this research, if only to know that there are others who feel as we do and know what we know.

Helpful or harmful effects of research participation

When asked what they had hoped for from participating in the interview, 7 of 10 expressed a hope that their participation would contribute to knowledge about perinatal loss:

I hoped that I would contribute to bringing the experience of pregnancy loss out of the closet and help make it possible for women like myself to speak openly and to have this experience of motherhood acknowledged and validated.

Like this woman, many spoke of how they had decided to grant an interview because they hoped their stories would help "others" to understand the effects of perinatal loss. "Others" included not only parents who suffer a loss, but medical practitioners and society in general. The hope was that by sharing their feelings and their stories they could contribute to an easier path for other parents or improve service delivery by others. Their losses would count for something. In the previous chapter, I discussed how parents sought to create some good from their experiences by informing others and by sharing their experiences and how this was one way that parents could salvage some meaning from their loss. The interviews provided just such an opportunity, and they may have offered participants the opportunity to work on this part of their grieving.

Participants were also asked directly whether participation had been helpful to them. Eight of 10 people felt that participation had been beneficial. Universally, they cited that they needed to talk it through, that they had never been so open in their discussion, and that talking their loss through in this way had helped them to put things in perspective. Again, the interviews provided them with opportunities to "Review and Remember" and to "Revive and Reexperience the Feelings" in ways that are typically not available to parents with perinatal losses.

Discussion

The responses I received in the follow-up survey left me feeling fairly satisfied that I had provided parents with a forum for reaching a new level of understanding of their losses and that participation had not harmed most participants or impacted negatively on their relationships. One woman, however, did give me considerable cause for concern with her responses:

> I found things coming out of my mouth I did not expect. I had never been so totally open about my feelings and explaining what happened. I had never discussed my reasons for being hospitalized, not even with my husband. It brought up feelings of anger and depression. I also started having nightmares again. I was reliving all the feelings all over again.

This woman had a particularly difficult experience, got very little support from her husband, family, workplace, or community, and was briefly hospitalized postpartum for a psychiatric assessment because her doctor feared she might commit suicide. In telling her story, she was able to make the connections between her lost career, her isolation, her struggling marriage, her present feelings of depression, and her child's death. In a subsequent discussion, she described how, after the interview, she began to realize that she had a number of secondary issues to work through. She describes how this knowledge came about:

> I attended the candlelight ceremony at the Children's Hospital, and as I stood there, I looked around and I realized, "This is not what this is about any more. This is not about my baby—this is about something else." And I thought about all the things we'd talked about and all the

things I've lost, and I realized that I have to come to terms with those things, too. So maybe it's time to work on them, too.

Although I cannot say with certainty that participating in the research has helped this woman, it did change her insights regarding her situation, and it has resulted in her seeking outside help to work on her grief.

I believe that this woman's situation, in particular, is a compelling argument for conducting a follow-up study when researching sensitive issues. If I had not done a follow-up study, I would never have known how profoundly the interview had affected her, triggering old and new feelings. I responded to her questionnaire by speaking with her on the phone several times (she included her return address on the survey form) and, with her permission, made a referral to a helping professional. I have continued to hear from her as she confronts her losses. Unlike Ebaugh (1988), who suggests researchers would be best advised to steer clear of emotional terrain by redirecting questions or by shifting to a more neutral tone (p. 224), I do not believe that simply changing the subject is adequate when dealing with people's emotions. On the contrary, I believe it is a moral obligation for interviewers to respond directly to respondents' calls for help and then, if possible, make the necessary referral. To do otherwise would, I think, be unethical.

In my discussion on research methods (see Appendix A), I stated that I chose to use Rando's model to expand my analysis because I wished to develop a model for "clinical sociology." There is significant overlap between the research interview and the clinical/therapeutic interview. As a sociologist, I feel compelled to acknowledge this juncture and respond to it in ways that are responsible and humane, that is, by honoring my respondent's feelings and by providing ongoing support for those who were made vulnerable by their involvement in this project.

COMING FULL CIRCLE

I began this research, like many of the people who responded to the follow-up survey said, in the hope that I could put some perspective on my own loss. In reality, my reasons for participating were the same as other participants: I wanted to share my knowledge, I wanted to learn something about how others dealt with loss, and I wanted to have the deaths of my children serve some meaningful purpose—I wanted to make a difference.

As I have transcribed the tapes of my interviews, I have had the opportunity not only to listen to the words and tone of others, but I have also had a chance to hear my own development over time. It has struck me in hearing these tapes how my language has changed. In early interviews, I myself refer to "miscarriage" rather than "death of your baby" or "when...died." I had intended from the outset to use language that would not minimize the nature of perinatal loss, but during the course of those early interviews, and perhaps reflecting my own minimization of my children's deaths, I slipped into language that did just that. As the interview tapes proceed, it becomes clearer and clearer that I am talking about death, not a medical mishap; that I am talking about trauma, not just a bad experience; that I am talking about babies, not fetal products.

I found interviewing others to be a powerful vehicle in my own healing. Hearing people say out loud things that I had only admitted to myself (and even then, not always) was extremely legitimating. So many of the regrets parents have revolve around feeling that they have not done enough to save the baby or have not fought the medical establishment hard enough or have failed to honor the baby's death adequately. As I heard myself tell people how little they could have changed things or how difficult it is to fight for what one needs in the middle of a desperate situation or how impossible it is to know in advance what one can only know in hindsight, only as I heard my assurances to others that what they had done was the best that could have been done under the circumstances, only then did I learn that those things were true for me, too. Through feeling compassion for others in their pain and helplessness and anger, I came to have some compassion for my own pain, helplessness and anger.

In one later interview, a woman tearfully admitted that she had not named or buried her daughter. She spoke of how sorry she felt for "abandoning" her child's remains and how she regretted not having honored her child's death adequately. In turn, I told her how I had never buried my children either, and how I have felt terrible guilt about that. I told her how difficult it is to know what to do in these situations because as parents we receive so little guidance from those who are in a position to inform us as to what we "should" do. I told her it was never too late, and if she wanted to name her child now, or plant a tree to create a place where she could symbolically bury her child, she could do that now, too. I told her how, just 2 weeks earlier, I had planted a tree in my garden to commemorate the young lives lost years before. I told her to forgive herself. And as I said those things, I began to forgive myself, too. I understood that I, too, had not been given enough guidance or support in negotiating my loss—that I had not done "better" at grieving simply because I was never shown how.

After a particularly insightful interview with a woman who has been very open in discussing her dead child with her two living children, I finally went home and invited my only living child to discuss her feelings of loss. I lost my babies when my daughter was 3 and then 4 years old. I had always wondered how those terrible experiences had affected her, yet I had never brought the subject up directly, perhaps subscribing to the social norm that these things were better left alone. I invited her to explore my own little bundle of baby mementoes—something she had never done before. We looked at the photographs and marvelled at the tiny footprints and discussed how sad it is that she will never have a brother or sister with whom to share her life. I cried a little, and so did she, and then, in her infinite 10-year-old wisdom, she reached out and placed her hand on my shoulder, saying, "You know, Mommy, you should have done this a long time ago." And she was right. It was as though some terrible secret had been released.

Several months later, when she had to give a presentation at Girl Guides on her family, by her own choice, she took that little package with her and publicly claimed her own relationship to her little siblings. It seems 10-year-olds are adept at creating memories, too.

As for her father, well, it seems more difficult to find some kind of positive meaning with him. At the end of this long project, and many, many heartfelt talks later, we are finally able to turn our gaze on the past without flinching. Maybe we will never be able to see what "good" losing our babies has meant to us as a couple, but at least we can now say that their deaths are a part of our shared history and that they are real to us in a way that was not possible before I undertook this research.

A final outcome for me is that by doing this research I have already touched the lives of many people and have been privileged to have made a difference in their grief process.

I began this project seeking to understand how bereaved parents find new meaning and wisdom through the trauma of losing a baby. I end it with my own transformation; by doing this research, I, too, have become a wiser person and have been granted the opportunity to find new and powerful meanings in the deaths of my own children. It may seem ironic, but today I can honestly say that I am grateful for the legacy Victoria and Evan have left in my life. I am blessed.

Chapter 8
Epilogue

After my first tentative decision to take on this research, I came home, stood in my garden and was overwhelmed by my feelings. It was a moment of epiphany. I felt both terrified and elated. Those feelings played themselves out during this research in a number of ways.

The initial terror came from an intellectual place for me. I felt humbled and frightened by the thought that I could be responsible for unleashing some powerful new way of seeing perinatal loss. If what I "discovered" was beautiful and helpful, then it would be a great accomplishment. If it was horrible and hopeless, perhaps this was research best left untouched. Either way, I fully believed in my power to create Truth, and my responsibility as a researcher for that Truth was enormous.

Emotionally, the power of such a worldview was increased for me because of my personal relationship to the research topic. If I chose to do this research, I would be opening up my previous self-knowledge to information that might not coincide with it. I might learn that this thing that I had been living was not real or important to anyone but me. I might learn that I had, indeed, been feeling and doing it all wrong. I might find out that losing a baby was, after all, not such a big thing. Finally, I was well-indoctrinated; I worried that if I were emotionally involved with the topic I might not be able to learn anything from what others told me. I might care too much to do real, valid research.

This combination of terror and joy was a constant companion to me while I did this work. Again, the impact was twofold: I was challenged both emotionally and intellectually by the work.

Many, many times after an interview I came home and wept. That was neither surprising or upsetting. However, other times I came home feeling angry or baffled or cynical. These feelings came up when I was confronted by people whose stories stood at the extreme ends of the continuum of experiences my participants shared with me. On the negative end, the man who steadfastly blamed his wife, for example, spoke out some of my own darkest thoughts. He gave expression to the voice within me that told me that I had been responsible, that I was to blame. Conversely, women who had serenely accomplished their mourning in the arms of a supportive family and community raised issues of how inadequate my own social support network had been. Other women, who had been so careful to advocate for themselves and who had been so creative in performing their own rituals, raised issues of my own inadequacy.

These were hard things for me to hear. These were the worst things, indeed, that I had imagined: that I really had been alone and abandoned by those in my circle who should have taken care of me; that I had, indeed, done it wrong and undervalued my own losses; that my mourning could have gone better if only I had been smart enough to do it differently. It seemed that others had known intuitively how to take care of themselves during this terrible time. That hit me right where my sense of competence lived—it seemed I was not so smart after all.

When I first began to hear those more positive interviews, I felt that I was dealing with people who must be either lying or crazy. I simply could not accept that others had found a way to live through this type of loss without being shattered. It hurt, yet I learned a lot from my pain.

I do not believe, for example, that I could have begun to write the chapter on Rando's six R's without learning, however painfully, about how some people managed to do some things right. When I listened to one woman in particular, an anthropologist who did many things to ritualize and make real her losses, my first response was to think that she was "over the edge." In the course of rethinking her interview—and it took me a long time to do that— I had to come to terms with my own assumptions about what was appropriate and good. I had felt so strongly about her rituals because I had been afraid to do anything like them. I had so internalized the norms of stoicism and individualism that I had come to manage my own feelings.

Ultimately, I tried some of the solutions that others had found helpful. I learned to be postmodern myself, taking things from interviews and encounters with other mourners, and bringing those acts in a personal way into my own life. Planting a tree, using the names of my children, talking to my husband, my child, my family and friends, making the loss real became ways for me verify my respondents' theories of "how to do grief" with a sample size of one. I lived the six R's while I did this project. And this is the joy that I referred to earlier.

Intellectually, there have been challenges and rewards as well. I learned experientially that although I operated in good faith and tried to do collaborative and constructivist research I was far from successful. I had hoped to do work that was empowering and that would involve people in the process. I had hoped to treat people with respect and honor. I believed that the interviews provided participants with an opportunity to bear witness.

However, constraints of time, money and energy resulted in research that was essentially postpositivist. In reality, the work has been my own project, enacted in isolation rather than in collaboration with others. Although my interviews were unstructured, and although I was respectful of my participants' need to tell their stories in an unconstrained and honoring way, I ultimately took their words home with me and did with them what I wished.

Even though I did not live up to the constructivist epistemological position, my belief in the constructivist ontological position has been strengthened. I am beginning to understand social research as a method of revealing new questions rather than providing final answers. I am beginning to accept that there is no Truth, but that does not mean that there is not something of worth to be learned.

I believe that this particular research has worth. Although I have not discovered "how perinatal loss is" or "how perinatal loss can be mediated," I have discovered "how perinatal loss can be" and "what has mediated perinatal loss for some." And that has profound worth to me and to the 10 women who responded to my follow-up survey with stories about how this research acted as an agent for change in their lives. It may not be truth with a big T, but it does have power—the power to change lives and illuminate people's experiences in ways that may not have been obvious before. And that is worth a great deal.

Appendix A
Methods—Investigating Perinatal Grief

RESEARCH DESIGN

The experience of perinatal loss is far-reaching, affecting people's lives on many different planes, yet little work exists in sociology or the social sciences that directly examines perinatal death in a way that encompasses gender roles, the concept of social death, disenfranchisement of grief or the impact of modern medical, familial, religious, community and employment structures on parental bereavement. This research project incorporates the varied theoretical perspectives explored in Chapter 1 to guide its approach in hopes of developing a more comprehensive picture of perinatal loss.

In addition to theoretical insights, this research is also guided by my own lived experience. My subjective experience provided the initial impetus for the study and informed much of the research direction. A growing body of sociological work calls for the researcher's subjective experience as a primary goal of interpretive research (Ellis & Flaherty, 1992). I have used my subjective experience as a jumping-off point and as a source of enrichment for my analysis of the perinatal loss experiences of others. Simply retelling my own story would not, I believe, provide a well-rounded representation of perinatal grief. I wanted to expand the picture to include women and men who held different ideas about mothering, about womanhood/manhood and about their feelings. Thus, I employed different qualitative research methods with a variety of participants in investigating this problem.

PARTICIPANT OBSERVATION

I attended several monthly meetings of Caring Beyond, a Calgary support group for parents suffering from perinatal loss. Caring Beyond is a volunteer-run organization that offers 24-hour telephone support and holds an open meeting once a month for parents who have suffered perinatal loss (which, in their pamphlet, includes miscarriage, ectopic pregnancy, stillbirth or early infant death up to 28 days after birth). They also perform community education to lay and professional groups and provide referrals to professional services for grieving parents.

Caring Beyond meetings are facilitated by volunteer parents, either as informal group discussions or as formal presentations offered by members of the medical, mental health, religious, or funerary professions. These presentations are then followed by open group discussions. Parents sit in a circle in a large, open room and speak when they feel the need. Volunteers reflect back on what participants say or open the floor to others for feedback. The meetings, held at the Children's Hospital, generally last about 2 1/2 hours and involve 30 to 40 participants, most of whom are female (the ratio of females to males was approximately 4-to-1 most evenings).

I did not take notes or tape record the meetings due to the nature of the sharing that occurred in these meetings, the constraints of recording technology and the effects of notetaking on group spontaneity. I did make extensive field notes when I got home following the meetings.

I also participated in a Parent Interaction Group sponsored by Caring Beyond. Parent Interaction Groups are intensive discussion groups that occur outside of the regular Caring Beyond meetings. The Group focus is:

1. To recall the parent's own loss experience;
2. To discuss the impact of the loss on the relationship;
3. To explore how the environment responded to the bereaved parents; and
4. To discuss various coping skills which can be useful in completing the grief work. (Caring Beyond Workshop Materials, no date)

The Parent Interaction Group I attended took place over two 3-hour evening sessions, and was attended by myself, two married couples and two female facilitators. Again, I did not tape record or take notes during the Interaction Group; however, I made extensive field notes following each session.

At the beginning of Caring Beyond meetings and of the Parent Interaction Group, I made known my dual role as participant and researcher by outlining my personal interest in the topic, the purpose of my research, my commitment to the anonymity of the group, my willingness to leave at any time if participants felt uncomfortable with my dual role, and an invitation for participants to question me on my research to date. No one objected to me either privately or in the group setting; in fact, many people made a point of expressing their support that this particular topic was being given much-needed attention by this researcher.

Focus Group

I conducted a focus group during a field trip to Medicine Hat. One woman in Medicine Hat responded to my initial newspaper call for participants, and as a result of that contact, I travelled there to interview several individuals. Medicine Hat is a small community, and the perinatal loss support group there is very close-knit. A number of people wished to participate in long interviews, but because of time constraints this was not possible. Thus, I opened participation to include a group situation, in part because I did not want to leave people out (I managed to achieve minor celebrity status in my 3-day visit), and also because I hoped a group dynamic might generate some new insights into perinatal loss. My contact, who is also a volunteer in the support group, coordinated the selection of focus group participants. We decided that a variety of different loss histories would be desirable, and the group selected was finally composed of five women and one man whose losses ranged from within the past year to 11 years ago, and it included one set of twins born at 20 weeks up to a full-term infant who died during birth.

The purpose of this group was to explore specific feelings and the situations in which those feelings occurred. The emotions that were discussed included: guilt, anger, shame, sorrow, loneliness, and fear. The group was encouraged to comment on what feelings came up, how those feelings occurred, in what types of interactions and settings they arose, and how their feelings were responded to by others. As group facilitator, I introduced each of these feelings with a brief definition of that emotion and how it had been mentioned by other people or in the literature on bereavement as a possible feeling attached to grief work. I then opened the floor to participants, ensuring that all members of the group were included in the discussion. This session was tape-recorded and the record transcribed. I also took field notes following the focus group meeting.

INFORMAL INTERVIEWS AND PERSONAL WRITINGS

I conducted a number of informal interviews with both professional and lay people working in the area of perinatal loss, read a variety of materials aimed towards parents who have suffered loss, and viewed two videos used as training materials for medical and mental health staff at the Grace Hospital. Finally, two women provided me with copies of journals and poetry they had written following their loss.

All of these elements, the support group meetings, the Parent Interaction Group, the focus group, the discussions with health workers, the reading materials, the journals, and the videos, converged to inform my understanding of the parental loss experience. The primary body of data, however, came from 25 intensive, semi-structured interviews with men and women who have suffered perinatal loss.

Long interviews

I chose to conduct long, unstructured interviews in order to accomplish two goals. First, I wished to understand perinatal loss from the perspective of parents themselves. The use of intensive, semi-structured interviews is one of the most powerful methods of qualitative inquiry, allowing researchers to "step into the mind of another person, to see and experience the world as they do themselves" (McCracken,1988, p. 9). Thus, to develop an understanding of the subjective experience of others, long interviews were an appropriate research instrument.

Second, I wished to offer parents the opportunity to speak out on their losses so that they might contribute to the growing public awareness and discourse surrounding perinatal loss. I felt that the simple act of being asked to tell their stories would be an empowering experience. Interviews can act as a way to bear witness, enabling people to name their injuries and connect with others by breaking silence (Riessman, 1993, p. 4). This second goal of the research complements a burgeoning self-help movement of grieving parents who make public their stories as a way to enlighten others and legitimate their right to grieve (Layne, 1990, p. 71).

My focus was to understand how parents create some sort of meaning and understanding out of their losses. From a symbolic interactionist point of view, meaning and understanding are not accomplished in a vacuum but are assumed to arise out of individuals' experiences that are grounded in social interaction (Charmaz, 1980). Thus, "although death is a biological fact, what it [means to] us results from our socially shaped ideas and assumptions" (Charmaz, 1980, p. 17). Some of the ideas and assumptions that influence perinatal grief include attitudes about motherhood and birthing, ideas about family and marriage, beliefs about death and spirituality, and cultural norms about responsibility, individualism, grief and mourning. I explored these ideas and assumptions in the interviews.

The interviews also explored interactions parents experienced both in public and intimate social arenas. Parents who have lost a child often find their personal experiences at odds with prevailing ideas and assumptions. These disjunctures are apparent in social interaction with a number of social institutions. Hospitals, physicians, medical technicians, nurses, funeral directors, insurance agents, social workers and clergy are all involved in death work (Layne, 1990; Letherby, 1993). For many parents, the death of their baby requires interaction with these institutions, often for the first time in their lives. Parents often learn appropriate grief responses through interaction with these institutions. In addition to these public and unfamiliar institutions, more intimate social institutions impinge on parents' private experiences. Immediate family, families-of-origin, friends, coworkers, and church and community members may provide interactions that help or hinder parents in their grieving (Letherby, 1993).

Explorations of parents' personal beliefs were also included in the interviews. A number of personal factors impinge on the process of grieving perinatal loss. Perceptions of womanhood, family pressures to provide children/grandchildren, beliefs about reproductive choice, religion, marriage, family, and life goals are all factors that can affect one's sense of self and one's decisions about bearing children; these also colour one's experience of losing a child.

I constructed a rather lengthy interview guide prior to beginning my research. A copy of the interview guide is included in Appendix B. Despite my careful construction, the actual interviews rarely followed the form of the guide. I conceptualized the interview structure along the lines of three overarching categories: what participants understood about perinatal loss prior to their own experiences; how their actual losses unfolded; and finally, what their subsequent experiences were in terms of interaction with others.

Often, once the preliminary questions about participant demographics and details regarding dates, ages and sexes of dead children were accomplished, participants would proceed to talk for 30–40 minutes uninterrupted, telling the story of their loss without pause. Participants were often extremely eager to talk about their experiences, perhaps reflecting a common lack of outlet for discussing their children's deaths. The challenge during these interviews was not one of prompting information from reluctant participants; rather, it became my work to use occasional, brief breaks to move the interview in one direction or another. Following the outpouring in the first stages of the interview, I would refer occasionally to the guide to flesh out particular areas that might have been glossed over or omitted by participants. Generally, however, my experience was that the interviews naturally unfolded to cover all the areas of interest I had conceptualized. I also was pleased that there were areas that I had not considered that came up during the interviews.

Interview sampling considerations

Researchers on perinatal loss have frequently recruited their participants from parental support groups, which can lead to a limited, white, middle-class bias in the sample (Layne, 1990, p. 71). I was extremely fortunate in enlisting the help of a local reporter, Susan Ruttan, who runs a daily column in the "Living" section of a Calgary daily newspaper, the Calgary Herald. In response to her one-paragraph call for participants, I received calls from as far away as Toronto (this woman's mother had cut out the article and mailed it to her). One woman in Medicine Hat wrote me to suggest an informant for inclusion in this sample. From that contact, I expanded my research base to Medicine Hat, undertaking five individual interviews, a joint interview with two women who had formed a support group, and a focus group for 6 parents (five women, one man) to explore their feelings surrounding perinatal loss. In addition to contacts obtained through the newspaper article, I conducted interviews with four people (three women, one man) who were recruited through Caring Beyond, a local support group for bereaved parents. Finally, interviews were conducted with three women who came to me through friends and acquaintances.

Besides broadening the sample beyond support group attenders, I sought to include men in my sample. Research to date has focused almost exclusively on women and their experiences of perinatal loss, and when men have been included, it has been as members of a couple rather than as individuals with their own grief issues. Although I did recruit my male participants primarily through their female partners, interviews were conducted with men and women separately in order to reduce the inhibitions that might arise in telling one's tale in front of a marital partner. Marital strain is a frequent accompaniment to the grieving process (Smart, 1992, p. 83) and differences in interpretation of the loss are part of that strain. I interviewed partners separately in order to obtain their particular, unedited interpretations of the loss and to avoid possible additional relationship strains that might arise out of joint participation in the interview itself.

Decisions for inclusion in the sample were determined primarily on participant willingness and availability. There are many different definitions of perinatal loss. Medical criteria consider pregnancy loss prior to 20 weeks to be a "miscarriage" and following 20 weeks to be a premature birth, criteria that are based on prospects of infant viability. Legal definitions of pregnancy also vary because death certificates are not in practice always issued, funerals are not always required, and life insurance is not generally paid out for perinatal deaths. Social criteria among acquaintances for pregnancy loss may depend on whether people have been told of the pregnancy or whether the woman "shows" her pregnancy. Criteria for partners and women themselves may vary: the feelings of movement, the first images on an ultrasound, a missed menstrual period, or a pink dot on a home pregnancy test may all represent points at which babies become "real" to their parents (Layne, 1992, p. 34). Rather than exclude someone from participating because of an externally imposed definition of "perinatal loss," I felt it was important to legitimate any parent's experience of loss if that was how that parent defined their experience. Thus, one woman who participated in this study experienced nine miscarriages, all of them during the first trimester of pregnancy. To exclude her on the basis of her not having suffered loss in advanced pregnancy seemed arbitrary; her story, particularly the story of her grieving, paralleled that of parents whose losses occurred at full term.

Interview context

During the interviews, I was open with participants about my own experience of loss. Most participants were recruited through a newspaper announcement that included a statement that I was both a researcher and a woman who had suffered her own losses. Other participants were recruited through Caring Beyond meetings, where I announced my presence both as a participant and as a researcher. A final group of participants were recruited through snowball sampling. These people were also informed of my dual role. This disclosure was a conscious decision on my part. Anne Oakley (1981) argues for abandoning the traditional criterium of maintaining distance in interviewing, saying, "The goal of finding out about people through interviewing is best achieved when the relationship of interviewer and interviewee is non-hierarchical and when the interviewer is prepared to invest his or her own personal identity in the relationship" (p. 41). I believe that informing participants of my own personal interest in and experience of loss gave me entrée to the topic that might not have been otherwise possible. As one participant said,

I felt a connection with the interviewer; I felt understood, and I knew I shared an experience with her that no one who has not experienced the same thing can fully understand.

I believe the understanding that arises from personal experience is invaluable in two ways: First, it enabled me to easily develop a rapport based on shared experience. People trusted me with their stories precisely because I shared at least some of what they had experienced. Second, my experience enabled me to guide the interview in a natural way, expanding upon what people said, or leading them in new directions without reliance on a research instrument. The flow of conversation was rarely interrupted or imposed upon by referral to the questionnaire.

Most interviews were conducted in participants' homes, four were conducted in my research office at the University, four were conducted in a hotel suite, and one was held in the participant's office. The general tone of the interviews was informal, warm and conversational. Interviews tended to be accompanied by coffee and cookies, and conversations generally continued beyond the formal interview. Often, lunch invitations followed the interview. Although most participants had young children at home, interviews were held at times when children were at preschool or when alternative childcare arrangements could be made. Interviews were also arranged at times when partners would be absent. I felt that in this way fewer interruptions and distractions would impose on the interviews. Nonetheless, for a number of women, such arrangements were not possible. Three women with infants breastfed their children while telling their stories; others let the dog in and out, tended to dinner, and fielded the curiosity of small children. Rather than detract from the quality of the interview, however, I felt this reflected comfort with me as an interviewer and with the research itself. Achieving such a comfort level goes beyond merely establishing rapport but contributes to the collection of more meaningful, comprehensive and honest information from participants (Oakley, 1981, pp. 51–55).

Almost without exception, people brought personal mementoes of their dead children to the interviews. There was a poignancy to these packages: often they included only a death certificate, some journal writings, or a packet of sympathy cards. But they were inevitably brought out during the course of the interview. As a researcher and as a mother, I struggled with my own feelings when presented with these mementoes. Maintaining cool distance and objectivity were neither possible nor desirable, but I also had to deal with my own feelings of sorrow and loss in order to honor the presentation of these mementoes. I learned to look at these pictures, footprints, cards and baby blankets without conjuring up my own personal images, but I still am not certain what the "right" response to these mementoes is. Ultimately, I simply looked and responded to what parents themselves had to say about this child's eyes or that one's nose or this card that came from some particularly thoughtful person.

ETHICAL CONSIDERATIONS

Prior to beginning each interview, I asked participants to read and sign an informed consent form. At the same time, I asked if they had any knowledge of Caring Beyond and supplied them with a pamphlet from Caring Beyond outlining the service provided by that group. I stated that I had no affiliation with Caring Beyond and that providing their information did not imply my endorsement of them. Included with Caring Beyond's hand-out was a listing of counselors in the Calgary area who are familiar with issues surrounding perinatal loss. I discuss the implications of this procedure more fully in Chapter 7, "Research as Therapeutic Process."

After participants had read the consent form, I paraphrased its contents for them: that their participation was voluntary and that confidentiality was ensured; how I would be storing and handling their data; and that I was willing to dispose of tapes and transcripts for whatever reason and at whatever time should participants so desire. I was very adamant that although I may have some particular questions or probes the interview was the participants' rather than mine, and they were welcome to refuse any question or to terminate the interview at any point. In addition, I stressed that there was no "right" way for the interview to proceed and that participants should feel free to explore and explain as they saw fit rather than worry about whether or not they had answered a particular question "correctly." No participant refused to answer any questions during the interview, all participants completed full interviews, and to date, I have not received any requests to destroy data or delete comments.

Interviews were audiotaped, and permission was obtained from participants prior to making recordings. People were offered the option of completing interviews while I took notes, but no one chose this option. One male respondent spent the first 15 minutes of our time together hooking my tape recorder up to his state-of-art system (complete with professional, floor-model microphone stand) rather than have his interview "turn out badly." The general impression I got was that people were fairly comfortable with having their words and stories recorded and were in fact eager to get through these preliminaries and on to the "real" reason for our meeting.

I always made sure I had Kleenex with me for the interviews. With the exception of two men and one woman, there were generally one or two

146

points in the interview when participants cried. There were several people who cried more or less throughout the interview. Perhaps because of my personal experiences, I did not find this emotional expression difficult or uncomfortable; in fact, I would have been surprised to find that people were not upset when discussing the deaths of their babies.

Ebaugh (1988) discusses strong emotion in research as a fairly common occurrence where "participants are hurting and reaching out to the interviewer as a fellow human being" (p. 224); however, she suggests that strong emotion is not something interviewers should attempt to deal with. She suggests interviewers redirect questions or deflect emotion by "asking a factual question which requires the respondent to give a rational response." Finally, she suggests that interviewers should learn to show their sympathy "by suggesting ways of getting professional help such as therapists and counselling services." I found this advice impracticable.

Perinatal grief becomes so painful for parents precisely because it is socially defined as pathological. Thus, when an interviewer responds to a parent's pain by suggesting therapy, she tacitly reinforces the social norms that define perinatal grief as abnormal. Further, to have the expression of one's feelings surrounding perinatal loss discouraged by changing the subject to something factual or neutral is, indeed, a fairly common social experience for grieving parents. People were willing—in fact, eager—to talk about their stories because nobody else had been willing to sit down and listen to them. If I, as a person specifically interested in perinatal grief, was not prepared to sit with them and fully explore their experience, including tears, I would be reenacting the very silence surrounding the subject that I wished to examine.

As a person who has known such pain, my struggle was not to avoid the pain of others; rather, my struggle was to not invoke my own feelings of sadness. I found it very difficult at times not to be moved by people's stories. In practice, when someone cried or found it difficult to continue, I often said very little. If I did speak, it was to assure them that crying was perfectly "okay" or that we could take some time here if they liked. Even with my acceptance of their emotional display, people often apologized for their tears as though such a thing were inappropriate.

INTERVIEW SAMPLE CHARACTERISTICS

I attempted to include as much variation as possible in terms of the gender and socioeconomic status of participants by going beyond support groups for participants. Twenty-one women and four men participated in long interviews, while five women and one man took part in the focus group.

The socioeconomic status of participants ranged from "poor" to "upper middle class." This measure was based on self-report; however, as most interviews were conducted in participants' homes, I was able to assess the apparent validity of their reports. Most parents fell in the lower middle to middle class range. Participants' occupations included several stay-at-home mothers, service workers, students, executives, and professionals. Education ranged from some high school completion to completed graduate/professional studies.

In this research, there were a number of other factors that I came to understand as being more important to sample makeup than education or socioeconomic status. Attitudes towards childbirth and family are intensely tied to issues of marital and gender socialization, religiosity, sexuality and pronatalism. I did not actively select participants on the basis of their reproductive histories or their philosophical orientation towards family and parenthood or on their religious or spiritual practices. Nonetheless, the final sample fortuitously included parents with various marital, occupational, religious and sexual practices, whose experiences encompassed a range of reproductive histories and family configurations.

Marital status

For the purposes of simplicity, and because all members described themselves as "married," whether their relationship was common-law, heterosexual or lesbian, I use the term "married" throughout when discussing an intact couple. The final sample included 4 men and 21 women. Two of the women were members of a lesbian marriage whose loss had followed a long round of artificial insemination attempts. The woman in the lesbian couple who did not bear the pregnancy responded in many of the same ways as the male partners in the sample did, so in many ways the gendered nature of her responses reflected a masculine, nonchild-bearing role. Of the 19 heterosexual women in the sample, all but one were in long-term relationships with the father of the dead child. Of those who were still together, however, two had separated for a period following the loss, one described her marriage as "somewhat intact," and over half described how their marriages had been precarious during the postloss period. Because males were recruited through partners, all of the men were heterosexual and in an intact marriage, and I was not able to talk to any men whose marriages were no longer intact.

Desirability of the pregnancy

Most of the people I spoke with described their pregnancies as having been desired, although there was one participant who clearly did not desire her pregnancy throughout her entire experience, and there were many women who described ongoing ambivalence during the first stages of pregnancy. It is possible that a wished-for pregnancy might be more painful to lose than one that is not welcomed by the pregnant individual herself. It is also possible that if the pregnancy is not socially acceptable, its loss will be treated with less sympathy and support. A single woman, for example, who experiences perinatal loss might feel social censure for undertaking a pregnancy and might find little support in grieving a pregnancy loss. Outside of the lesbian couple, I was unable to speak with anyone whose pregnancy had been deemed undesirable in the participant's social milieu.

Length of time since the loss

Because human actors are capable of reflecting on their own experiences and making choices in their interpretations of social events, those interpretations are not static but undergo ongoing change. Perinatal loss may mean different things to different people, and it may also mean different things to the same person at different points in their life cycle or at different points in their own grieving (Charmaz, 1980, p. 25). For this reason, respondents were included who were at varying stages of their reproductive lives, who had varying family sizes, and whose losses ranged from within the previous 6 months to as long as 29 years ago. It was hoped that by including people at various points in their grieving a broader picture of loss and recovery could be painted.

Number of losses and durations of pregnancies

I speculated that the number of losses a parent experiences might have a cumulative effect on parental grief. I also felt that the duration of pregnancies might affect both how individuals themselves view their loss and how the outside world responds to it. With advances in medical technology, parents become aware earlier and earlier of their pregnancies, however unchanged the outward signs of pregnancy remain. Thus, although parents might begin to develop attachments earlier, their social worlds can remain oblivious to the loss. I was interested in seeing how those disjunctures might affect parental grief.

The sample included women whose pregnancy losses were solely in the first trimester; women whose losses were "late-term miscarriages," occurring after the watershed 20-week mark; women whose infants died before or during labor; one man whose son had lived for 2 weeks; and finally, a man who, besides two perinatal losses with his present wife, had lost a child to Sudden

Infant Death Syndrome in a previous marriage. The number of losses experienced ranged from parents who experienced a single loss to one woman who had suffered nine losses. Nine participants had survived a single perinatal loss, while four had lived through four or more. In fact, over half of the sample reported having had more than one type of loss and were able to comment on the impact of those differences.

Reproductive history

There are many facets to one's reproductive life. One's age at the time of loss, the configuration of one's family, and previous reproductive actions that include abortion, adopting-out a child, or delaying having children all are likely impact on how one experiences grief. The age, particularly of the mother, can affect feelings about future children, while the number of children a parent has before and following the loss may impact on the experience of grief. The sample included parents who had no children other than the lost child, parents who had adopted, parents who had children before and after the loss, and four women who were pregnant at the time of the interview. There were three women in the sample whose most recent loss had been their final attempt to have a child, while several were still unsure whether they would attempt another pregnancy. The age of mothers at the time of their losses ranged from 22 to 38 years of age. There were also women included who had previous abortions, two women who had given children up for adoption, two women who had adopted children, and three women who had themselves been adopted. For the parents who had adopted children, as well as the lesbian couple who had become pregnant through artificial insemination, pregnancy loss was colored by fertility issues.

Career orientation

I speculated that one's attitude toward career might impact on grief. Women in the sample included both professional women and those whose primary orientation is towards raising a family and being a stay-at-home mother. Males in the sample were all career-oriented. Future research might want to consider the role of occupation in men's grieving processes as well: for example, it was not possible with this sample to explore whether being a stay-at-home father impacts heavily on men's grief.

Social support

I wanted to explore how people's experiences of loss and their creating of meaning were experienced within a variety of social frameworks, being guided by the symbolic interactionist understanding that meanings are social and are created through interaction with others. The sample included men and women who were in solid marriages, those whose marriages were precarious, and those whose marriages were socially marginal (e.g., inter-racial, common-law or lesbian couples). The sample also included people who were well-established and connected in the city, relative newcomers to Calgary, members of highly supportive church, lay and familial communities, and people who described themselves as having been isolated during their grieving.

Religion and religiosity

Different religions have differing philosophies regarding when life actually occurs and what happens after death. They also have differing practices regarding the care of the dead and the acknowledgement of infants as having lived or not. The sample included one Jew, four Catholics, one Catholic who also followed Buddhist teaching, two Anglicans, three United Church members, one Mormon, five evangelical Christians, seven people who claimed no particular religious affiliation, and one woman who was clear that she was an "atheist, not an agnostic."

I speculated that religiosity, the degree to which one adheres to the tenets of a religion and the amount of involvement one has in a religious community might have an effect on how people interpreted their losses. The sample included the wife of an evangelical Christian Minister, two daughters of missionaries, a number of people who attended church "once in a while," several people who were raised in a particular church but who no longer attend, and a few who had never been connected to any religious community.

DATA ANALYSIS

All interviews were tape recorded and transcribed by me, following the recommendations of Mishler (1986). He discusses the interview as a conversation between two people rather than a simple question-and-answer undertaking. The paralinguistic elements of conversation—comments, pauses, interruptions, sighs—are as important to the content of the interaction as the actual words. My transcriptions included notes about pauses that indicate struggling over a concept, the tone of voice, the laughter or tears in order to make note of critical contextual issues in the interviews. Mishler also discusses the dilemma of the interview: that it is not merely a stimulus-response paradigm to be simply coded and readily understood as measures of specific concepts. Often, long interviews unfold as narrative events, and the order of that unfolding may not fit a rigid interview guide. This was certainly my experience of interviewing; participants were as "in charge" of the interview as I was, and their narratives, although perhaps more difficult to analyze in all their messy, random glory, cover far more ground than would have been obtained by adhering to a rigid interview schedule.

The analysis for Chapter 2, "How Perinatal Loss is Experienced," was conducted according to grounded theory methods, where themes are drawn out of the data itself (Charmaz, 1983; Glaser & Strauss, 1967). In grounded theory research, data analysis proceeds inductively, with data collection, analysis and research occurring simultaneously. I began interviews in February of 1995 and completed my final interview at the end of August, 1995. During that time, transcription of earlier interviews was ongoing, as was my review of the literature, attendance at support meetings, and interviews with helping professionals in the field. Thus, my understanding of the problem evolved as I performed both field and theoretical research. As my understanding developed, I applied methods of theoretical saturation and theoretical sampling.

Theoretical saturation occurs when certain topics are continually repeated in the data without providing new insight. Once theoretical saturation has occurred, the researcher, in theory, goes on to explore new areas of the topic. This proved to be less cut and dried than the literature would imply; people's stories of perinatal loss were simply not constructed in such a way that I could ask them to "pass over" aspects of the experience that I felt had been saturated. I did, however, do less probing during later interviews in those areas.

Theoretical sampling refers to the process wherein the data collected sets new research directions. Perhaps an interview might point out some area of the problem that has been heretofore unconsidered. When this happens, theoretical sampling leads the researcher to seek out instances of that particular aspect in hopes of saturating that element of the problem. I was able to employ theoretical sampling throughout the course of my data collection as I transcribed and analyzed interviews at the same time as I continued interviewing. With each new interview, I was able to shift the focus slightly to explore aspects of the problem that emerged from previous data. For example, the inclusion of two lesbians in the sample came near the end of my study and was motivated by my developing understanding of the disjunctures between parents' social supports, their needs for legitimation and their right to grieve. I wanted to explore the situations of parents whose right to grieve was particularly unsupported by the community at large.

Another theme that emerged was the pain of experiencing discrepancies between expectations of support and actual support. I began to hear that this discrepancy was perhaps more salient than the actual quality of support received and that if one did not expect support its absence would be less painful. In later interviews, I included questions and discussion about disappointments and pleasant surprises when discussing social supports.

A third, overarching theme that emerged was that of transition. People described changes in relationships, in perceptions of others, in expectations, in beliefs and worldview and in self-knowledge. As the research progressed, I increasingly explored areas of change, asking questions about who people thought they had become, what relationships had changed, what beliefs had changed, how they reinterpreted their lives, and what those changes meant to them.

In Chapters 3, 4 and 5, my analysis was informed and organized using Therese A. Rando's complicated mourning theory. I came to Rando's work late in this project and was struck by how appropriate her model was to perinatal loss. Her theory is itself grounded since it has been developed in her clinical practice as a grief counselor.

Another rationale for using Rando's theory stems from my hope that this research will be useful not only for parents who lose a baby, but that it can be used as a model for professionals who help those parents. Rando's work is well-known in the world of clinical practitioners and is based on a well-developed understanding of the clinical implications of complicated mourning. Using a clinical model to guide my analysis seems an appropriate model that will be useful for practitioners who work with bereaved parents. In combining grounded theory with an established clinical framework, I hope to develop a model of "clinical sociology" that combines the insight of clinical practitioners with a sociological understanding of perinatal loss.

This combination of grounded theory and received theory has been argued for by other methodologists, for example, Strauss and Corbin (1994, p. 277), who note that trained researchers are theoretically sensitized whether they acknowledge it or not and that use of explicit theories can be fruitful when played against themes in the data. According to them, theoretical sensitivity is based not only on "disciplinary or professional knowledge, [but] research and personal experience" (1994, p. 280). I believe that I brought all these elements to my analysis of the data: grounded theory that emerged from an inductive analysis of the data, an appropriate application of

Rando's theory to expand and organize themes, and my own personal experience to add depth of understanding to the analysis.

Appendix B
Interview Guide for
Semi-Structured Interviews

Before we begin to discuss your miscarriage, I would like to gather a little information about you which might be useful in my research. Please be assured that this information is not designed to identify you in any way. All the information you give me will be held in strict confidence, and your anonymity is assured. I also want to assure you that we can skip any questions which make you feel uncomfortable, as well as add in anything which you think should be added. Is that okay with you?

I. BASIC PERSONAL INFORMATION (Approximately 10 minutes)
1. What is your age? What was (were) your age (s) at the time (s) of your miscarriage (s).
2. What is your relationship status (single, married, in a same-sex relationship, common law, other—specify)
3. What was your relationship status at time of miscarriage (s)?
4. What is your occupation?
5. What is your level of completed education?
6. How would you describe your social class at present?
   At the time of your miscarriage?
7. Do you practice a religion?   Specify_____If yes, would you classify yourself as minimally, fairly, or highly "active" in your church?

Now, we can start dealing with questions about your miscarriage. I want to try to break this experience down into a sequence of before, during and after your mis-carriage. I would like to hear about your experience during those different periods, but I hope to focus most of our discussion on your experience after the miscarriage. Please understand that this is a flexible interview, however. If you want to tell me something, or if you feel one of these questions triggers something else, please go ahead with that thought. I am going to start with the period which occurred before your loss. Are you okay to go ahead?

II. BEFORE THE MISCARRIAGE (Approximately 10-15 minutes)
8. What was your knowledge of miscarriage before losing your baby?
9. Did miscarriage come up as a topic in childbirth classes?
10. Was miscarriage discussed by your physician?
11. Had you ever talked or known about miscarriage before through your mother, or other relatives?
12. Had you ever talked or known about miscarriage through friends or acquaintances?
13. Did you think miscarriage was possible or likely in pregnancy?
14. Did you have any feelings about miscarriage before your own? Could you try to tell me what they were?

Now I want to go on to the time of the miscarriage itself. For now, I would like to talk about the immediate experience, but if something is triggered for you, please go ahead with that thought or feeling. Are you comfortable with that?

III. DURING THE MISCARRIAGE (Approximately 20-30 minutes)
15. Please tell me about your own experience, and the feelings you had, <u>at the time</u> of the miscarriage in your own words.

Note: The following are some follow-up questions which I will use should my particular interests not be addressed by this open-ended approach:

How long ago did your miscarriage happen?
What was your status at the time (married, single, etc).?
Did you have any other children at the time?
Was this a planned pregnancy?
Did it occur more than once? Explain.
Where did the miscarriage occur?
Were you alone?
If not, was someone personally connected to you there?
    Who?
    Were they helpful? How?
    Were they difficult? How?

If not, was someone professionally related there?
Who? (Dr., nurse, social worker, clergy, eg.)
Were they helpful? How?
Were they difficult? How?

Now I would like to talk about what happened to you after the baby was lost. I want to go through some of the ways that you were or were not able to grieve, and what some of the outcomes have been for you personally. Please feel free to add anything you think is important, to take your time in going through these questions, or to stop at any time. Are you okay to proceed?

IV. AFTER THE MISCARRIAGE (Approximately 30-45 minutes)
16. Please describe for me what your feelings were after the miscarriage.
Note: The following feelings are ones which I hypothesize will be mentioned spontaneously. These questions will be posed only as probes if necessary.

Please tell me whether these feelings are something which you experienced:
•guilt (describe the times you felt this way, and why you think you felt this way)
•shame (describe the times you felt this way, and why you think you felt this way)
•loneliness (describe the times you felt this way, and why you think you felt this way)
•responsibility (describe the times you felt this way, and why you think you felt this way)
17. Sometimes different feelings are attached to the different roles we fill. For example, we may have different feelings when acting as a wife/husband than when we are acting as a parent. Think of some of the roles you find yourself in, for example, as a woman, as a wife, as a parent, and tell me what the effect of the miscarriage was on your feelings about those roles.

Note: the following roles are those which I hypothesize will intersect with the experience of miscarriage for individuals. These will be posed only as probes if necessary:

•as a woman/man?
did you feel your womanhood/manhood was affected? How?
•as a parent?
did you tell your other children?
did you have to comfort other children, for example?

---

tell me about how that went
•as a potential parent?
did you think you would never have other children?
did you try again?
tell me about that?
•as a partner?
what were some of the effects on your relationship with your partner?
tell me about your feelings in this area.
•as a daughter/son?
what feelings, if any, did you have towards your parents or your partner's parents?

18. I am going to name some individuals, groups and settings which might have provided a response to your miscarriage. Please tell me what their response was, and what your feelings were about that reaction.

a. Please describe the response after your miscarriage from the Medical community. What were your feelings about that?

(following are hypothesized responses and feelings. These will be used as follow-up if necessary)
•answers as to the cause of the miscarriage, or future implications?
•support?
•legitimating (a sense that what you had gone through was real, important)? explain.
•any follow-up—medical or emotional?
•feelings of being ignored, minimized, discomfort on the physician/nurse's
part
•positive and negative experiences
•did you feel alienated, angry, isolated, ashamed? misunderstood?

b. Please describe for me the response you encountered from your partner. What were your feelings about that?

(following are some hypothesized responses and feelings. These will be used as follow-up if necessary.)
•discussion or silence?
•blame?
•support?
•differences in grief?

•anger? from the partner? from you?
•guilt?
•did you feel alienated, angry, isolated, ashamed? misunderstood?

c. Please describe for me the response you encountered from your church. How did that make you feel? (if no church, go to next question)

(following are some hypothesized responses and feelings. These will be used as follow-up if necessary)
•support/solace?
•minimizing/compounding the problem?
•did this affect your relationship to the church?
•if so, how?
•did you feel alienated, angry, isolated, ashamed? misunderstood?

d. If you have no church affiliation, have you ever considered whether that may or may not have been helpful? Please explain.

e. Please describe for me the response you encountered from your neighbors. How did that make you feel?

(following are some hypothesized responses and feelings. These will be used as follow-up if necessary):
•public gestures of support? (flowers, cards, food)
•private gestures of support? (talk, offers to babysit, eg.)
•negative or just neutral?
•how long did support last, if at all?
•did you feel it was adequate?
•did you feel alienated, angry, isolated, ashamed? misunderstood?

f. Please describe for me the response you encountered from your family (outside of your partner and any children) How did that make you feel?

(following are some hypothesized responses and feelings. These will be used as follow-up if necessary):
•public gestures of support? (flowers, cards, food)
•private gestures of support? (talk, offers to babysit, eg.)
•negative or just neutral?
•how long did support last, if at all?
•did you feel it was adequate?
•did you feel alienated, angry, isolated, ashamed? misunderstood?

g. Please describe for me the response you encountered from your friends. How did that make you feel?

(following are some hypothesized responses and feelings. These will be used as follow-up if necessary):
•public gestures of support? (flowers, cards, food)
•private gestures of support? (talk, offers to babysit, eg.)
•negative or just neutral?
•how long did support last, if at all?
•did you feel it was adequate?
•did you feel alienated, angry, isolated, ashamed? misunderstood?

h. Please describe for me what happened at your workplace, if applicable. How did that make you feel?

(following are some hypothesized responses and feelings. These will be used as follow-up if necessary):
•time off? explain.
•cards, phonecalls, home or hospital visit?
•how did long support last, if at all?
•did you feel it was adequate?
•did you feel alienated, angry, isolated, ashamed? misunderstood?

i. If applicable, please describe for me your interactions with other children living at the time of your miscarriage. How did it make you feel?

(following are some hypothesized responses and feelings. These will be used as follow-up if necessary):
•a help or hindrance in your dealing with grief?
•were you open or not about your miscarriage with them?
•did they act out at all? How?
•how did that impact on you?
•how did that impact your partner?

19. Support Group—did you attend one?
yes/no?
why/why not?
If yes,how long?
was it positive/negative?
did you come right away?
why/why not?

•Is (are) there any area (s) where you sought help that I have not mentioned?

•Describe your experience with that support

•Are there any experiences which you feel I have missed that were particularly meaningful for you in this experience?

Personal Responses

Please tell me whether you felt any of the following:
    •Need for information, answers? Were you able to get that? If so, How?
    •Need to talk? Were you able to get that? If so, How?
    •Need for silence? Were you able to get that? If so, How?
    •Permission to be sad? Were you able to get that? If so, How?
    •Need for acknowledgement. Were you able to get that? If so, How?
    •Need to avoid. Explain who you needed to avoid, and why.
    •Need to confront (medical, silent spouse, eg.). Were you able to do that? Explain.

How has your life been changed since the miscarriage? For example, could you tell me about:
    Changes in attitudes—explain
    Changes in beliefs—explain
    Changes in lifestyle—explain
    Changes in relationships—explain
    Changes in occupation or life-goals—explain

Have you done any of the following:

    •Used any object (like photos, clothes) or ceremony to commemorate your lost child? Please describe the object/rite. Was that helpful?
    •Done any writing on the subject. Was that helpful?
    •Done any reading on the subject. Was that helpful?
    •Attended any support groups. Was that helpful?
    •Attended any public rituals, like the candlelight ceremony at Caring Beyond or the Graveside Service during the Summer. Was that helpful?
    •Made any decisions which you regret?
    •Made any moves, breaks in your routine, changed jobs, etc., because of the miscarriage? What was the impact of those decisions?
    •Did any relationships change because of your miscarriage. Please tell me about that.
    •Did any relationships end because of your miscarriage? Please tell me

about that.
•Did you ever withdraw, because of the miscarriage?
•Did you ever feel suicidal because of the miscarriage?
•Did you ever attend therapy because of the miscarriage? Was that help-
ful? Please tell me about your experience.
•Did you ever worry that you were grieving inappropriately?
•Did you ever worry that you might be losing your mind?
•Did any old unresolved issues arise as secondary issues?
•Did anything good come out of the experience? Explain.

*I appreciate your insights. One final area I want to explore is your feelings about
the future. Could you share with me what some of the impacts are on your future
choices?*

Impact on reproductive decisions
   •have you discussed sterilization? Explain.
   •have you discussed adoption? Explain.

Impact on subsequent pregnancies
   •have you taken on subsequent pregnancies? Explain.
   •will you take on subsequent pregnancies? Explain.

Impact on subsequent children.
If you have borne children subsequent to your miscarriage, how has it
affected:
   •that pregnancy
   •your relationship with the new child
   •your grief over the lost child

*I want you to know how much I appreciate your willingness to share this experi-
ence with me. I realize that it is very difficult to do so. It is possible that I might
need to do some follow-up work with you in order to clarify certain points, or to
make sure I am understanding properly what you have told me. Would you be
available for follow-up? Thank you again for your time and candor.*

Bibliography

Aries, P. (1985). *Images of man and death*. Cambridge, MA: Harvard University Press.

Arnold-Hagan, J., & Buschman, G. P. (1983). *A child dies: A portrait of family grief*. Rockville, MD: Aspen Publications.

Badinter, E. (1980). *The myth of motherhood: An historical view of the maternal instinct*. London: Condor Books, Souvenir Press.

Bauman, Z. (1993). *Postmodern ethics*. Oxford: Blackwell Publishers.

Charmaz, K. (1980). *The social reality of death: Death in contemporary America*. Reading, MA: Addison-Wesley Publishing Company.

Charmaz, K. (1983). The grounded theory method: An explication and interpretation. In R. M. Emerson (Ed.), *Contemporary field research: A selection of readings* (pp. 109–126). Boston: Little, Brown & Company.

Cook, J. A., & Wimberly, D. W. (1983). If I should die before I wake: Religious commitment and adjustment to the death of a child. *Journal for the Scientific Study of Religion, 22*(3), 222–238.

164

Denzin, N. K. (1989). *Interpretive interactionism* (Sage Applied Social Research Methods Series 16). Newbury Park, CA: Sage Publications.

Doka, K. H. (1987). Silent sorrow: Grief and the loss of significant others. *Death Studies, 11*, 455–469.

Doka, K. H. (1989). Disenfranchised grief. In K. J. Doka (Ed.), *Disenfranchised grief: Recognizing hidden sorrow* (pp. 1–13). Lexington, MA: Lexington Books.

Ebaugh, H. R. Fuchs (1988). *Becoming an ex: The process of role exit.* Chicago, IL: The University of Chicago Press.

Ellis, C. (1991). Emotional sociology. In N. K. Denzin (Ed.), *Studies in symbolic interaction: A research annual* (Vol. 12, pp. 123–145). Greenwich, CT: JAI Press Inc.

Ellis, C., & Flaherty, M. (1992). An agenda for the interpretation of lived experience. In C. Ellis & M. G. Flaherty (Eds.), *Investigating subjectivity: Research on lived experience* (pp. 1–13). Newbury Park, CA: Sage Publications.

Fowlkes, M. R. (1991). The morality of loss: The social construction of mourning and melancholia. *Contemporary Psychoanalysis, 27*(3), 529–551.

Gittins, D. (1993). *The family in question: Changing households and familiar ideologies* (2nd ed.). London: The MacMillan Press Ltd.

Glaser, B. G., & Strauss, A. L. (1967). *The discovery of grounded theory: Strategies for qualitative research.* New York: Aldine de Gruyter.

Hai, D. M., & Sullivan, D. H. (1982/1983) The silent sympathy: A study of attitudes toward spontaneous abortion. *International Quarterly of Community Health Education, 3*(1), 79–91.

Hochschild, A. R. (1983). *The managed heart: Commercialization of human feeling.* Berkeley, CA: University of California Press.

Hochschild, A. R. (1987). Ideology and emotion management: A perspective and path for future research. In T. D. Kemper (Ed.), *Research agendas in the sociology of emotions* (pp. 117–140). Albany, NY: SUNY Press.

Layne, L. L. (1990). Motherhood lost: Cultural dimensions of miscarriage and stillbirth in America. *Women & Health 16*(3/4), 69–89.

Layne, L. L. (1992). Of fetuses and angels: Fragmentation and integration in narratives of pregnancy loss. *Knowledge and Society: The Anthropology of Science and Technology, 9*, 29–58.

Letherby, G. (1993). The meanings of miscarriage. *Women's' Studies International Forum, 16*(2), 165–180.

Littlewood, J. (1993). The denial of death and rites of passage in contemporary societies. In D. Clark (Ed.), *The sociology of death: Theory, culture, practice* (pp. 69–84). Oxford, England: Blackwell Publishers.

Lofland, L. H. (1985). The social shaping of emotion: The case of grief. *Symbolic Interaction, 8*(2), 171–190.

Lovell, A. (1983). Some questions of identity: Late miscarriage, stillbirth and perinatal loss. *Social Science and Medicine, 17*(11), 755–761.

Malcolm, N. E., & Wooten, B. L. (1984). *A beginning.* Toronto: Women's College Hospital.

McColm, M. (1993). *Adoption reunions: A book for adoptees, birth parents and adoptive families.* Toronto: Second Story Press.

McCracken, G. D. (1988). *The long interview* (Sage University Paper Series on Qualitative Research Methods 13). Newbury Park, CA: Sage Publications.

Mishler, E. G. (1986). *Research interviewing: Context and narrative.* Cambridge, MA: Harvard University Press.

Mulkay, M. (1993). Social death in Britain. In D. Clark (Ed.), *The sociology of death: Theory, culture, practice* (pp. 31–50). Oxford, England: Blackwell Publishers.

Oakley, A., McPherson, A., & Roberts, H. (1984). *Miscarriage.* Glasgow: Fontana Paperbacks.

166

Oakley, A. (1981). Interviewing women: A contradiction in terms. In H. Roberts (Ed.), *Doing feminist research* (pp. 30–61). London: Routledge & Kegan Paul Ltd.

Orbach, S. (1978). *Fat is a feminist issue.* New York: Berkeley Books.

Palmer, C. E. (1991). Human emotions: An expanding sociological frontier. *Sociological Spectrum, 11,* 213–229.

Rando, T. A. (1984). *Grief, death and dying: Clinical interventions for caregivers.* Champaign, IL: Research Press.

Rando, T. A. (1992). The increasing prevalence of complicated mourning: The onslaught is just beginning. *Omega, 26*(1), 43–49.

Rando, T. A. (1993). *Treatment of complicated mourning.* Champaign, Illinois: Research Press.

Rappaport, C. (1981). Helping parents when their newborn infants die: Social work implications. *Social Work in Health Care, 6*(3), 57–67.

Reinharz, S. (1988). Controlling women's lives: A cross-cultural interpretation of miscarriage accounts. *Research in the Sociology of Health Care, 7,* 3–37.

Riessman, C. K. (1993). *Narrative analysis* (Sage Qualitative Research Methods, Vol. 30). Newbury Park, CA: Sage Publications.

Schwiebert, P., & Kirk, P. (1989). *Still to be born: A guide for bereaved parents who are making decisions about their future.* Portland, OR: Perinatal Loss Press.

Smart, L. S. (1992). The marital helping relationship following pregnancy loss and infant death. *Journal of Family Issues, 13*(1), 81–98.

Strauss, A., & Corbin, J. (1994). Grounded theory methodology: An overview. In N. K. Denzin & Y. S. Lincoln (Eds.), *Handbook of qualitative research* (pp. 273–285). Thousand Oaks, CA: Sage Publications.

Taner Leff, P. (1987). Here I am, Ma: The emotional impact of pregnancy loss on parents and health-care professionals. *Family Systems Medicine, 5*(1), 105–111.

Tedeschi, R. G., & Calhoun, L. G. (1995). *Trauma and transformation: Growing in the aftermath of suffering*. Thousand Oaks, CA: Sage Publications.

Thoits, P. A. (1987). Emotional deviance: Research agendas. In T. D. Kemper (Ed.), *Research agendas in the sociology of emotions* (pp. 180–203). Albany, NY: SUNY Press.

Veevers, J. E. (1980). *Childless by choice*. Toronto: Butterworths & Co. (Canada) Ltd.

Videka-Sherman, L., & Lieberman, M. (1985). The effects of self-help and psychotherapy intervention on child loss: The limits of recovery. *American Journal of Orthopsychiatry, 55*(1), 70–82.

Index

Hai, D., 2
Heaven, 114, 119
Hochschild, A., 6, 7, 63
Holidays, 80, 112
  (*see also* Christmas)
Hopes and dreams, 38, 41, 107, 114
Hospital experiences, 18, 26, 55–56, 76–78, 80

Identity, 37, 117
Incest, 43
Individualism, 48, 71
Innocence, 40
Insomnia, 86
Insurance, 8, 13, 19, 47, 80
Isolation, 53, 65, 70, 84, 129

Kirk, P., 2

Lactation, 87, 90, 93
Language and perinatal loss, 13, 130–131
Layne, L., 3, 4, 9, 26, 140, 141, 142, 143
Legal system, 79
Legitimation
  lack of, vii, ix
Length of life, 60
Length of pregnancy, 142–143, 148–149
Lesbian, 53, 147, 151–152
Letherby, G., 3, 140, 141
Lieberman, M., 2
Littlewood, J., 5
Lofland, L., 65
Lovell, A., 2

Malcolm, N., 2
Maternity benefits, 8, 13, 21, 65
Maturity
  lack of, 44, 47
McColm, M., 46
McCracken, G., 140

McPherson, A., 2
Meaning of the loss, 36, 119–120
Medical doctors, 26, 55, 85, 99
Medicalization, 2, 57, 72
Medicine as infallible, 3, 4, 71–72
Mementoes, 107, 132, 144–145
Mental health, 44
Mishler, E., 150
Mormon, 73–74, 108, 119
Motherhood
  and self-concept, 37
  as moral imperative, 4–5
  as status attainment, 4–5, 22
Mothers
  as active participants in death, 10, 17, 83, 88–90
  as "principal" mourners, 21, 88
  as responsible, 3, 24, 25
  (*see also* Sex roles)
Mourning
  definition of, 10–11
Mulkay, D., 6, 69

Naming the baby, 106
Need to talk, 21–22, 28, 102, 107, 124, 141–142, 146
New reproductive technologies, 3–4, 72
Number of losses, 149
Numbness, 16, 84, 101–102

Oakley, A., 2, 143, 144
Orbach, S., 31

Palmer, C., 6
Parenthood
  and responsibility, 45
  as expectation, 37, 42
Participant observation, 138–139
Perinatal loss
  as trauma, 9–10
  crosscultural meanings of, 2